ILLUMINATIONS

An original publication by Visionary Publishing, Inc.
302 South County Road, Suite 118
Palm Beach, Florida 33480

Introduction by Peny North.

ISBN 0-937223-01-8

Many of the paintings in this book are
available as notecards and large poster
reproductions. For more information and a free
catalog write to Visionary Publishing, Inc.,
302 South County Road, Suite 118
Palm Beach, Florida 33480

Printed in Hong Kong

ILLUMINATIONS

THE VISIONARY ART OF GILBERT WILLIAMS

For further information on Visionary art, limited edition lithographs, posters and notecards, please contact:

VISIONARY PUBLISHING, INC.
302 South County Road, Suite 118
Palm Beach, Florida 33480

ILLUMINATIONS

THE VISIONARY ART OF GILBERT WILLIAMS

When considering the origins of Visionary Art, some will look to the recent past of psychedelic art. Though they will discover a certain aspect of Visionary Art, they will hardly have reached the origins. Others, more knowledgeable about the history of various art movements, will look to the Surrealism of Hieronymous Bosch or the poetic images of William Blake. They will have come closer to the source, but the true origin of Visionary Art is with the origins of art itself. The earliest cave drawings excepted (for those paintings were language more than art), Visionary Art began when the message communicated was more than information. Visionary Art began when the message was intended to go beyond simple communication to inspire a greater vision.

Visionary art has existed for thousands of years, predating one of its first recognized forms, the Thangka Art of the Far East. The works of Bosch and Blake certainly are an integral part of what is called Visionary. However, the works of most of the Great Masters (though given differing names based upon time and technique) are also part of the elusive Visionary Movement.

To define Visionary Art, we must first consider the manner of expression and then the message expressed. The manner of expression is most simply defined as the incorporation of two or more disparate realities in the same image when these disparate realities are represented naturalistically. The message expressed is both positive and looking to the highest ideals of humankind. The message is a message of optimism above all others. Therefore, to be Visionary Art, a work must include at least two distinctly unique paradigms of reality represented naturalistically and expressing an uplifting message — containing a spiritual content.

Many of the Great Masters painted the confrontation of the mortal and immortal paradigms with the intentions of comunicating hope. Thus, many of the Great Masters were Visionaries.

After the works of Bosch and Blake, the Visionary artist re-emerged with the American Luminist or the Hudson River School artists. Sargent, Cole, Bierstadt, and (perhaps most notably) Church combined the "real world" of Earth and Nature with the more "surreal world" of Light (combining two disparate realities) in attempts to inspire a grander appreciation of each and both. Pioneers reaching beyond the known world to bring back "pictures" of what the future frontiers held, they took their viewers beyond the tangible world into a world of imagination that lay beyond. They blurred the boundary between these two worlds to suggest that we could have the best of either world — perhaps the best of both. These were the Visionaries of the turn of the century.

Contemporary Visionaries are also pioneers as they reach beyond our technologically hectic world into the worlds of imagination which lie beyond. They bring back "pictures" of what the future frontiers hold. They similarly blur the boundaries suggesting that we can have the best of either or both worlds. The contemporary Visionaries speak to people of hope, peace, and of greater possibilities and grander realities. With all the individual and global changes in our world, Visionary Art brings light to an often dark perspective — a light which may not be necessary for our physical survival, but which is essential for our mental, emotional, and psychic well-being. It is essential for our spiritual nurturement.

The leading Visionary Artist today is Gilbert Williams. His work depicts the fullest and truest meaning of the term more than many others who claim the label "Visionary". Yet Williams resists the label. He sees his work as simply an expression of his dreams, his hopes, his inner worlds of personal exploration.

Gilbert Williams is in many ways the quintessential Visionary painter. His canvases are filled with the imagery of transcendence — moons and temples, goddesses and gateways, groves and guardians, lakes and light beings — and a brilliance of light, color, intricacy, and beauty virtually unknown in contemporary painting. In paintings that range from ancient Celtic ring stones to Greek temples floating in space, each image points toward a deeper knowledge and even more beautiful possible realities. Though his originals usually go to collectors within days of completion, his images are nonetheless widely known. Visionary Publishing, Inc., publishes notecards, posters and lithographs of his work, and his images have also been seen on the album covers of Michael Jackson, Crosby, Stills & Nash, and the Fresh Aire albums by Mannheim Steamroller & The London Symphony. His paintings have also been used frequently as illustrations in **Omni Magazine**.

From an early love of drawing, Gilbert Williams explored art history and the techniques of the Renaissance Masters. Other studies included anthropology, archaeology and geology, culminating in an ever-expanding interest in metaphysics. Almost entirely self-taught as a painter, Gilbert Williams is one of the foremost Visionary artists in the world.

– Peny North
President, Illuminarium Gallery, Inc.
& Visionary Publishing, Inc.

CONTENTS

The Plates

1. ABODE OF THE PHOENIX

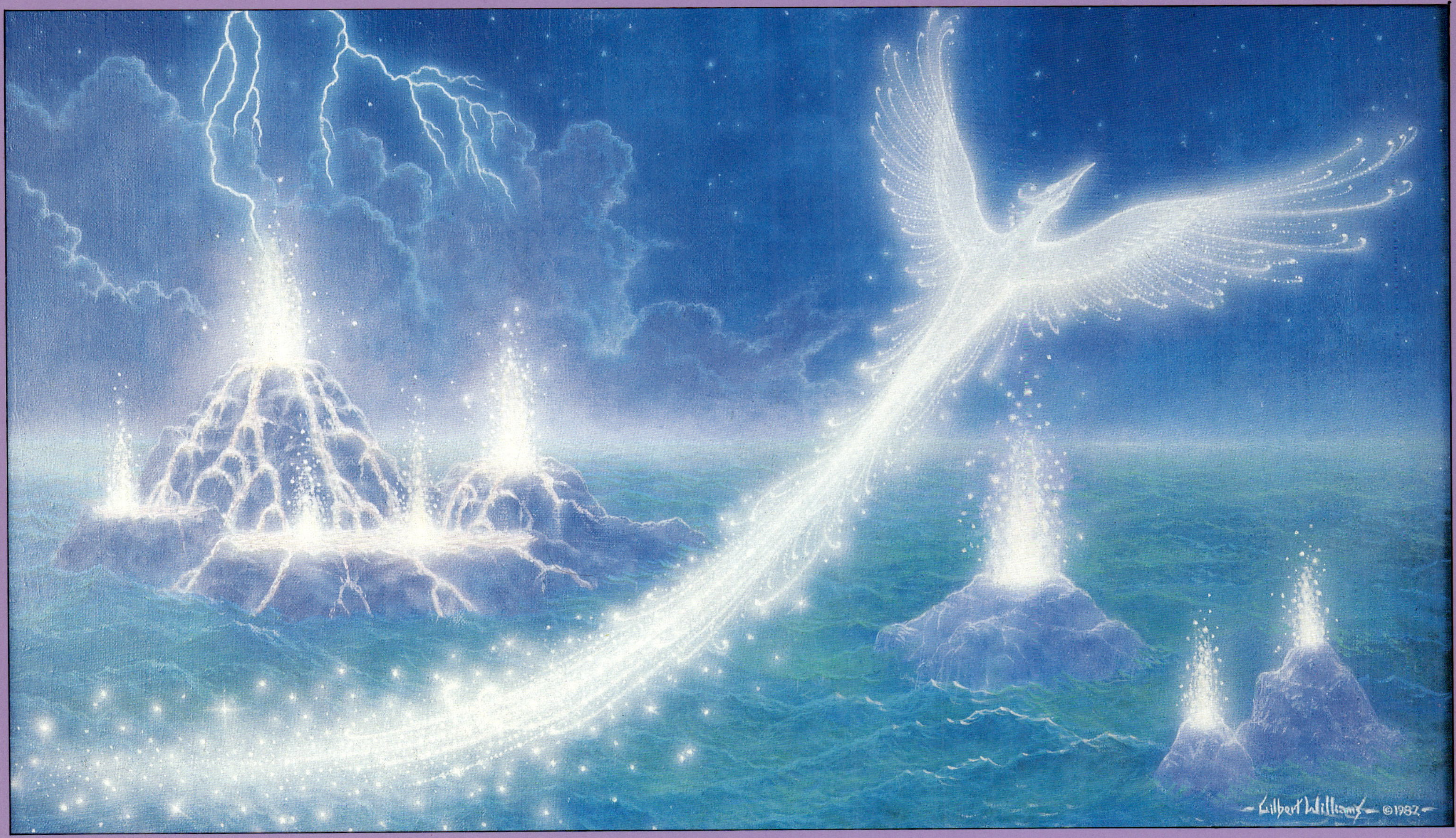
Gilbert Williams ©1982

2. AMETHYST

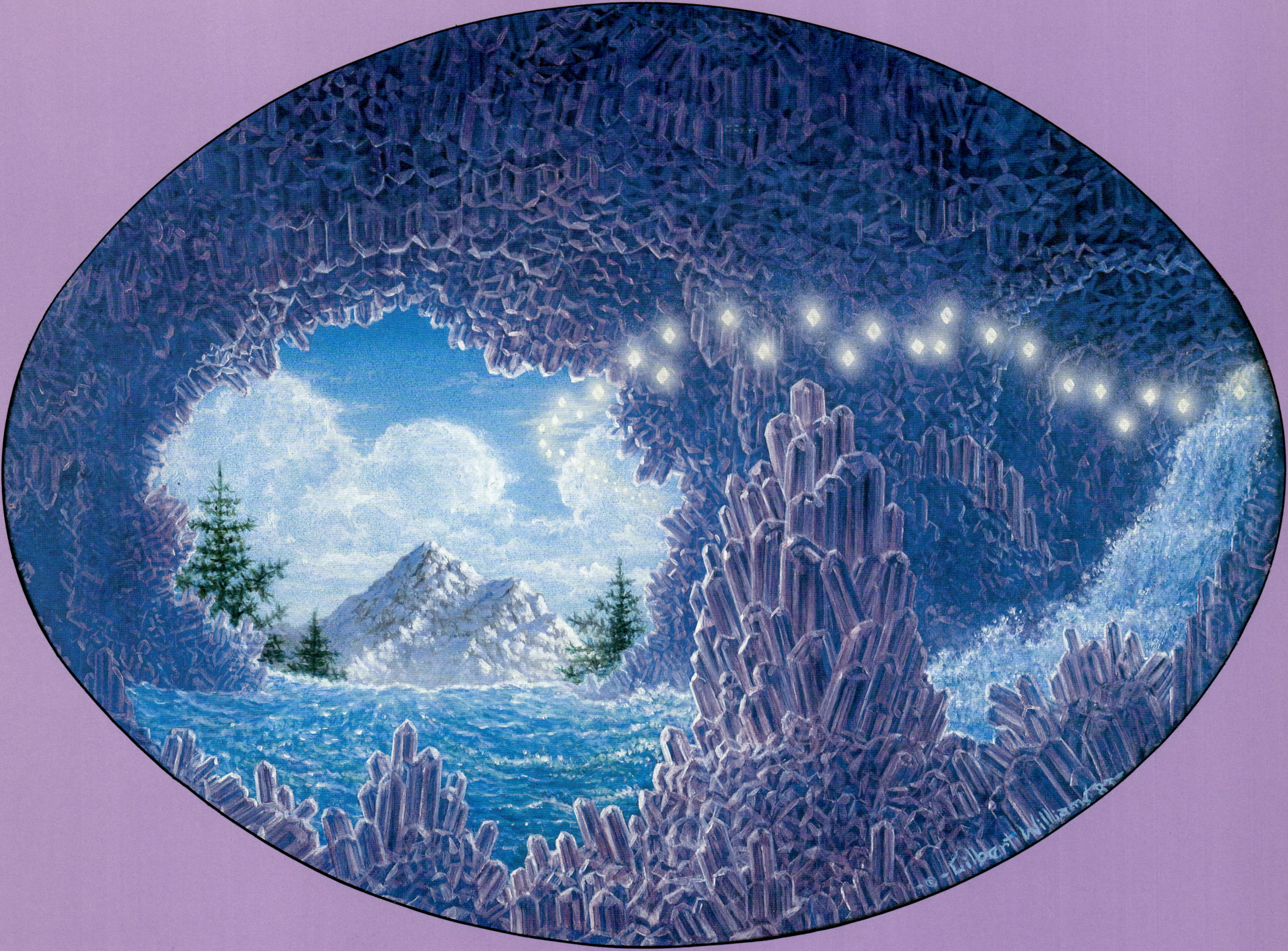

3. ANCIENT SHORES

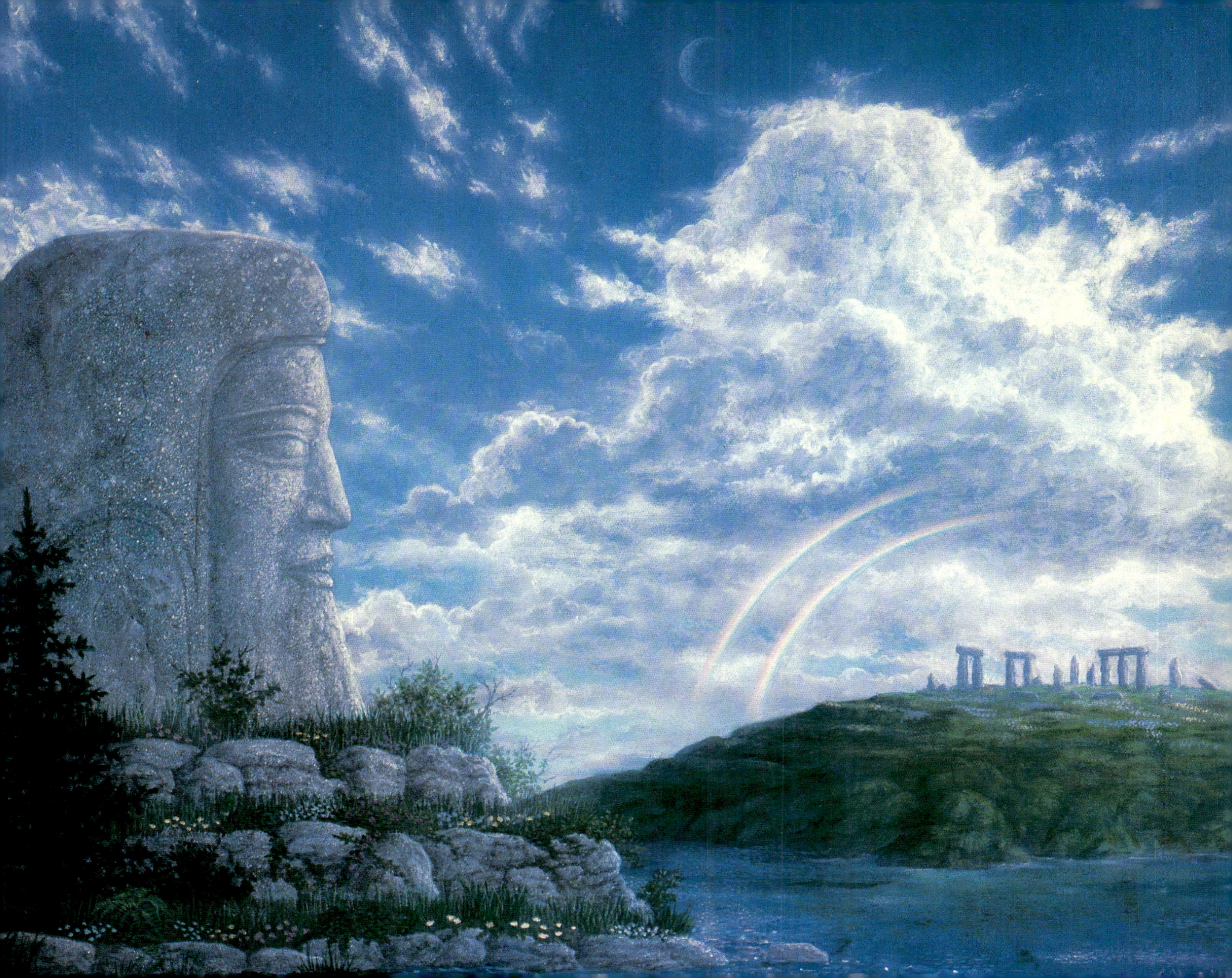

4. ANGEL FALLS

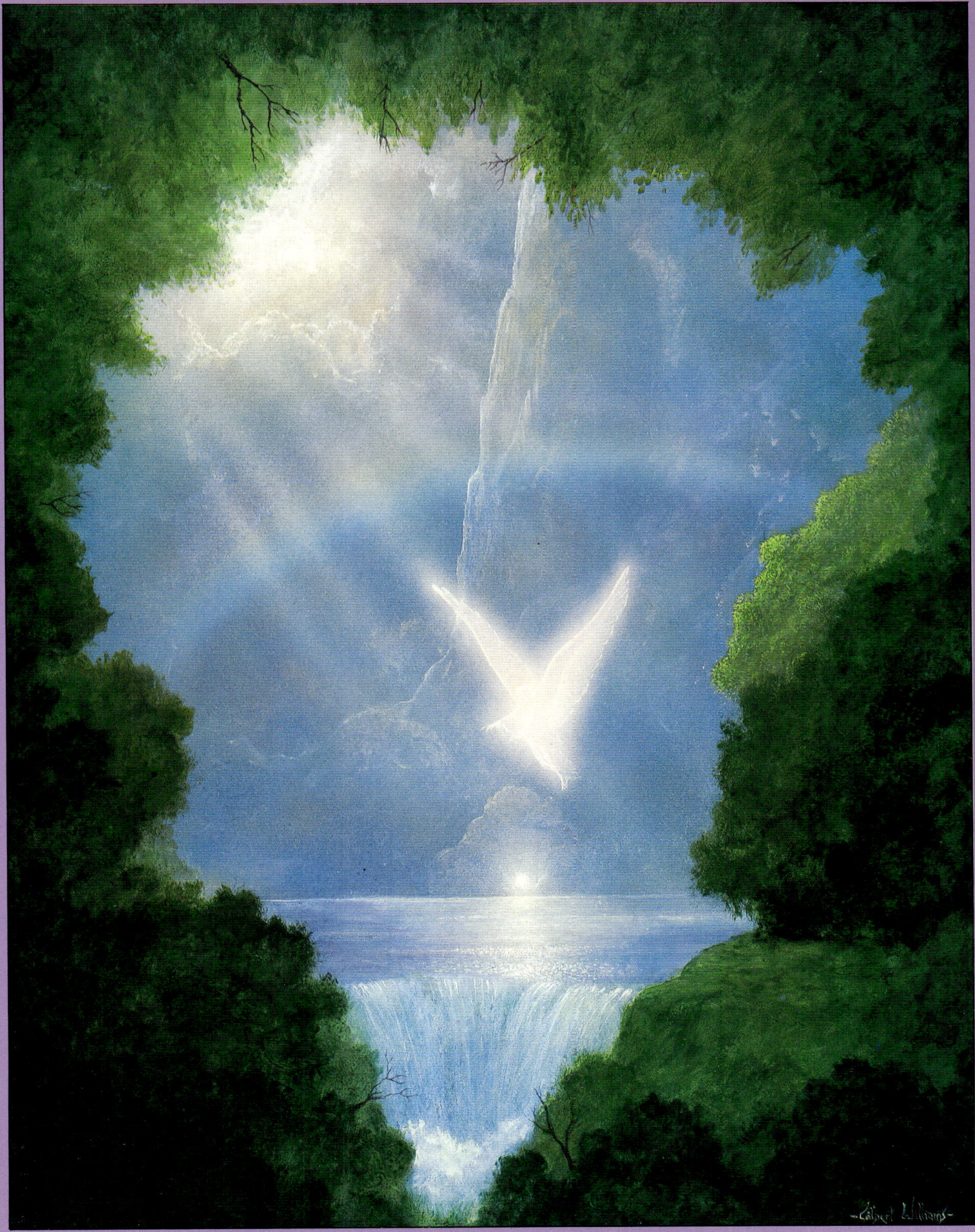

5. ANGEL LIGHT

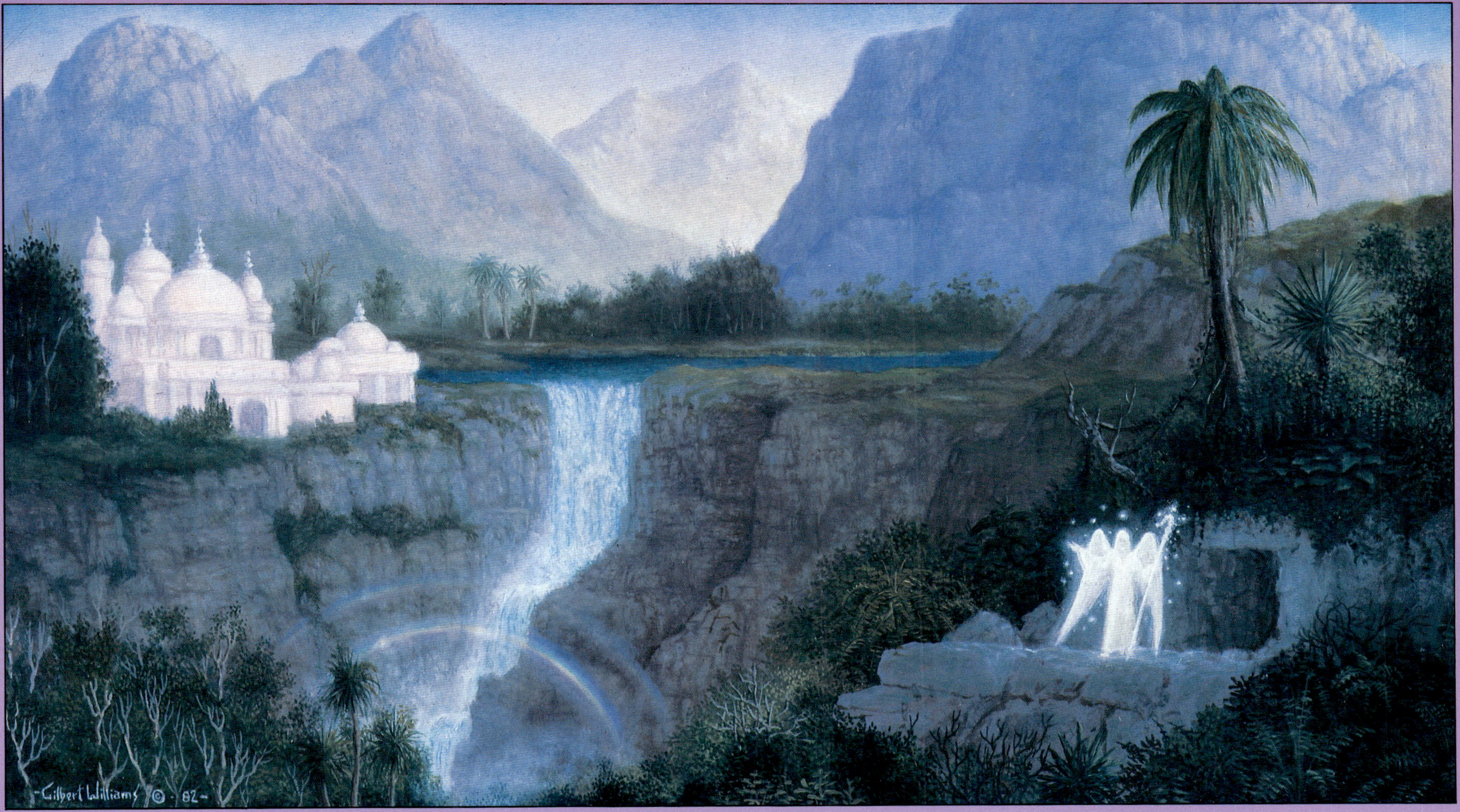
Gilbert Williams © 82

6. ARRIVAL OF THE CRYSTAL SHIPS

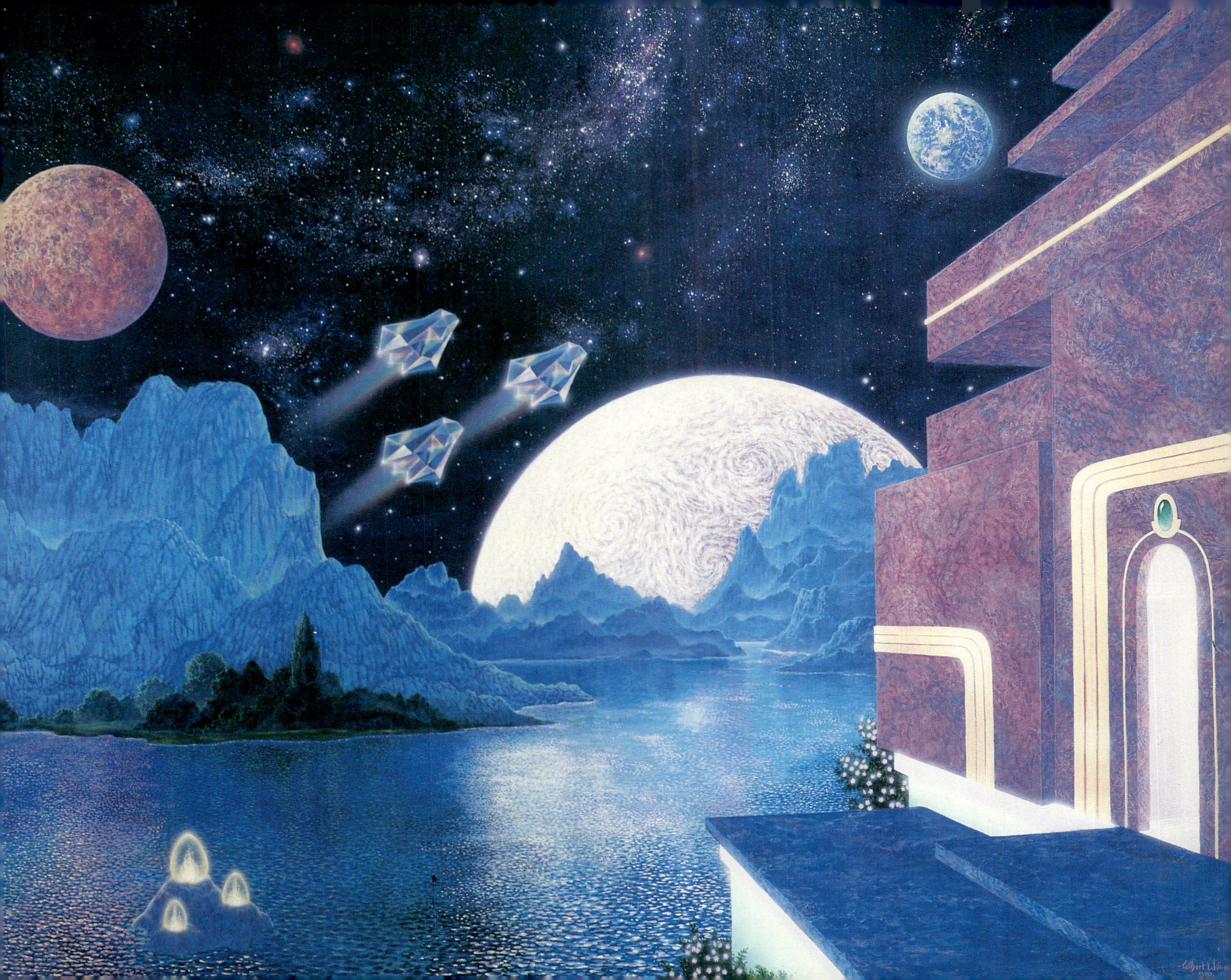

7. CAUSAL PLANE

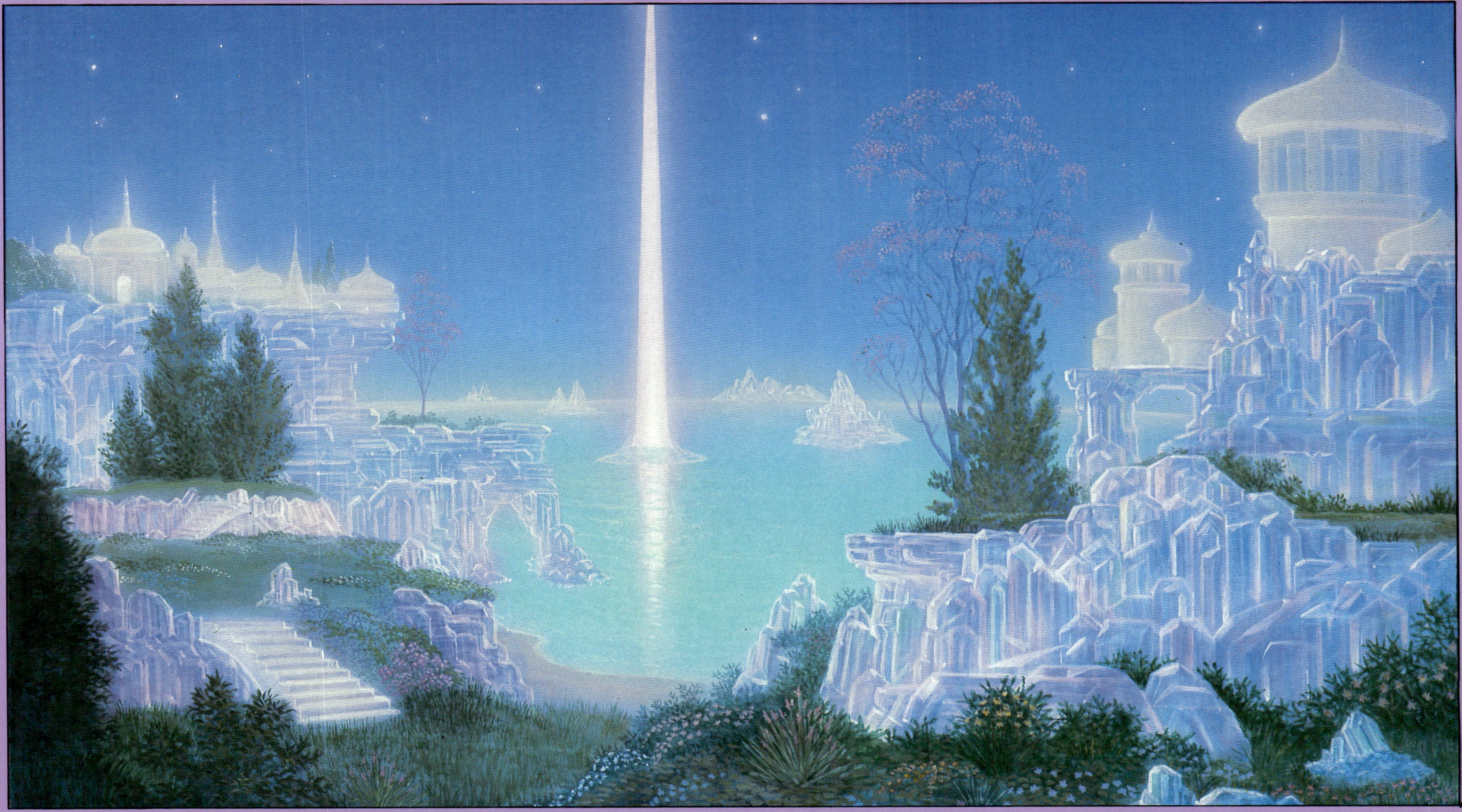

8. CHORUS OF THE DAWN

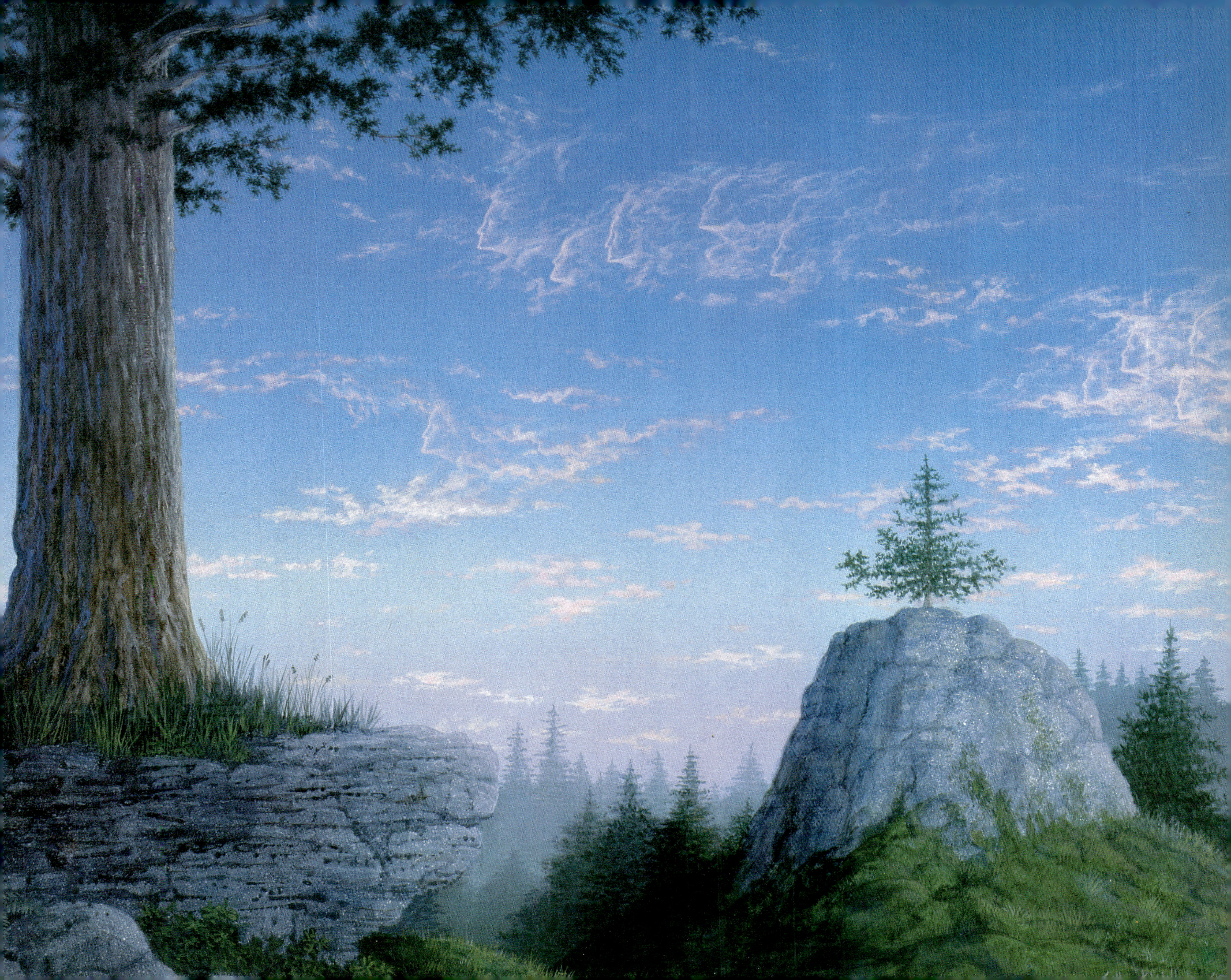

9. CITY OF LIGHTS

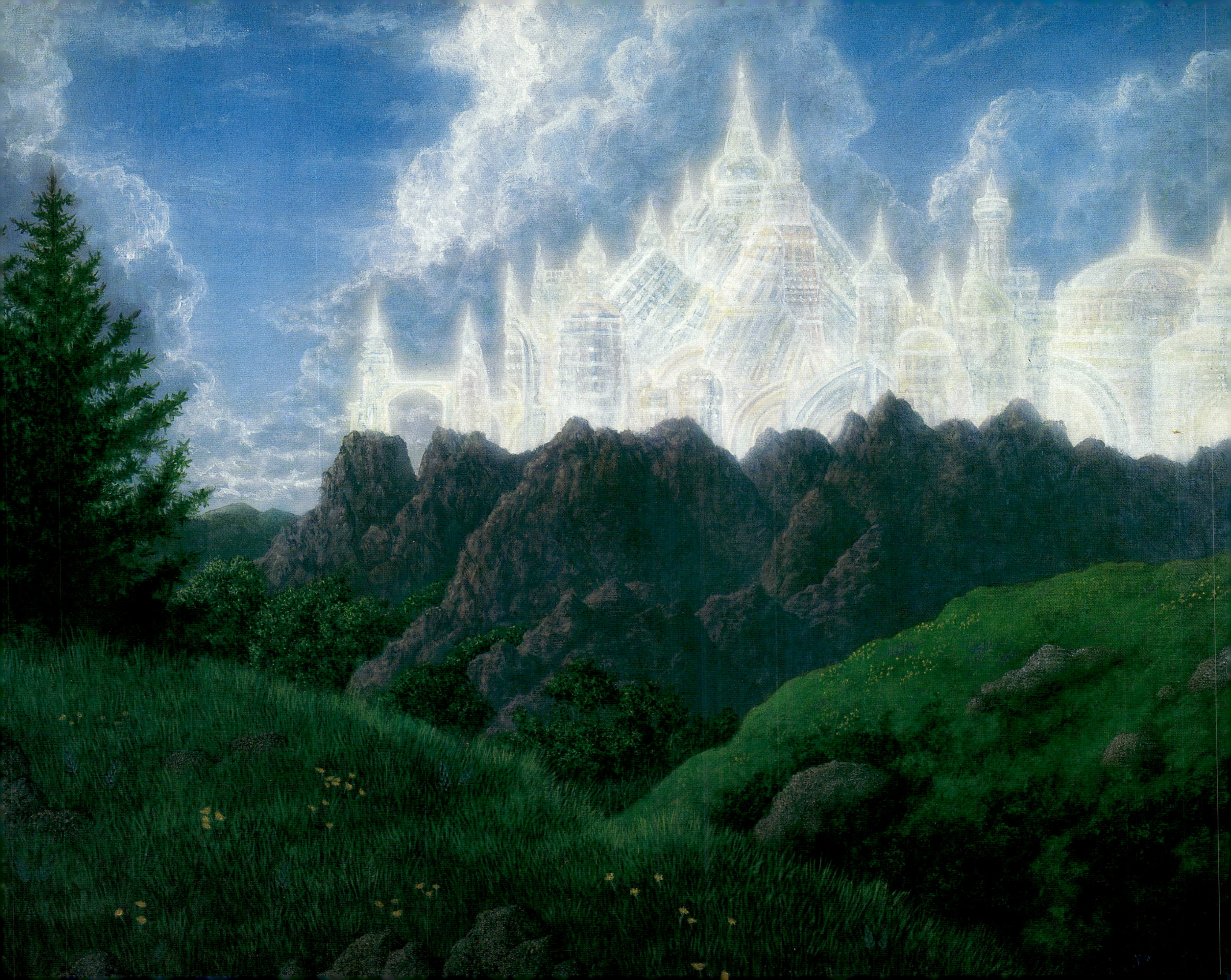

10. CLOUD CANYON

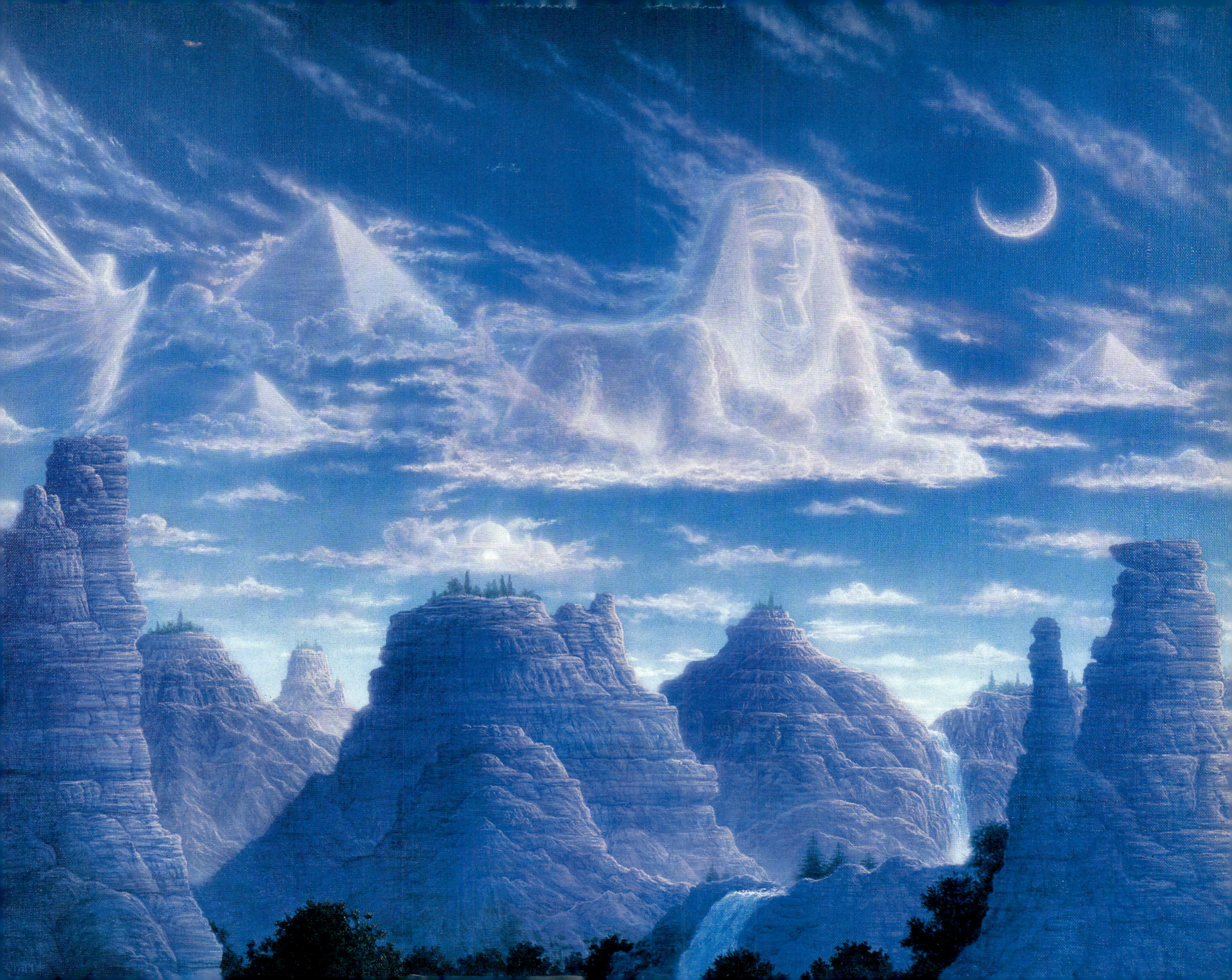

11. CONVERSATION

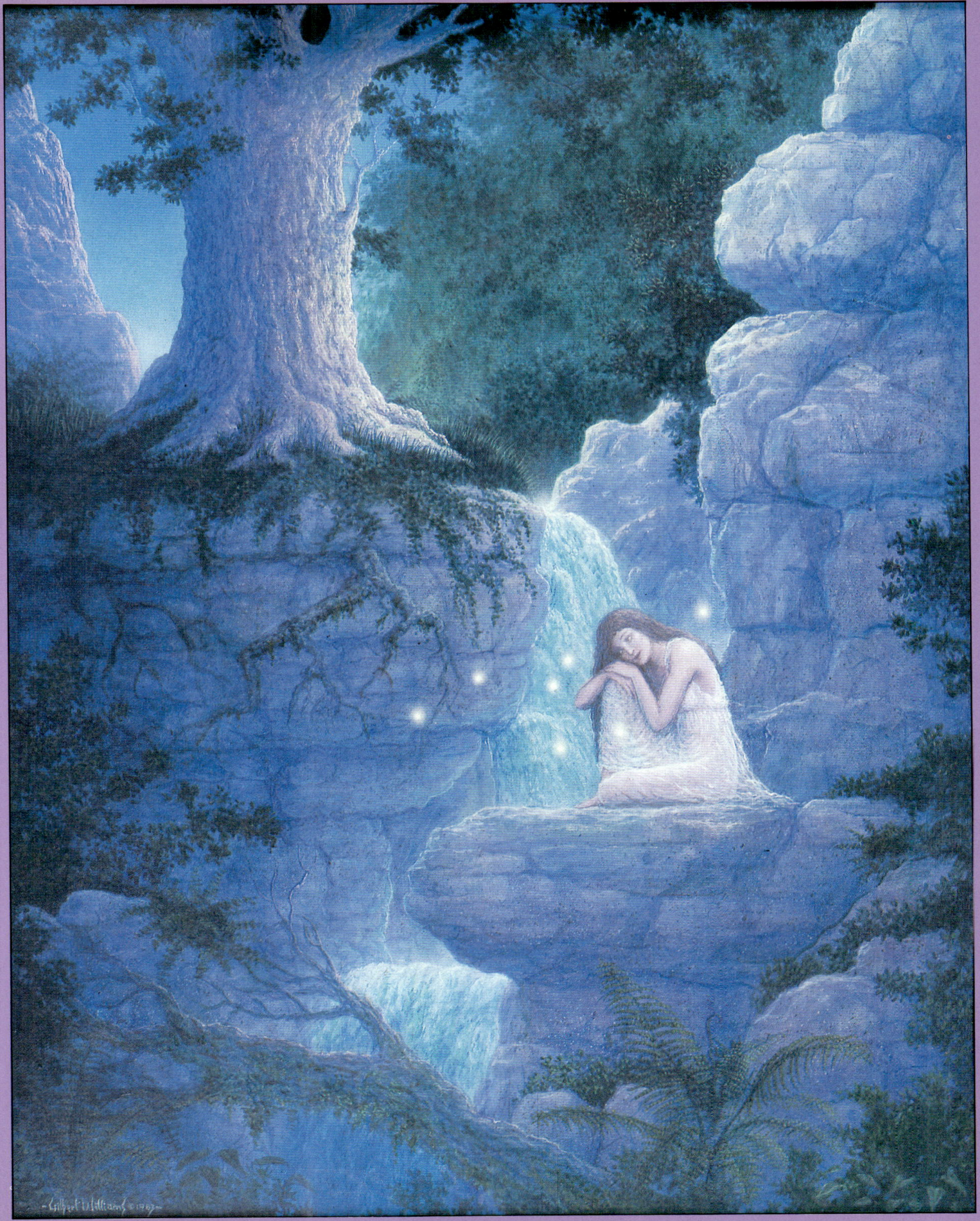

12. CRYSTAL PALACE

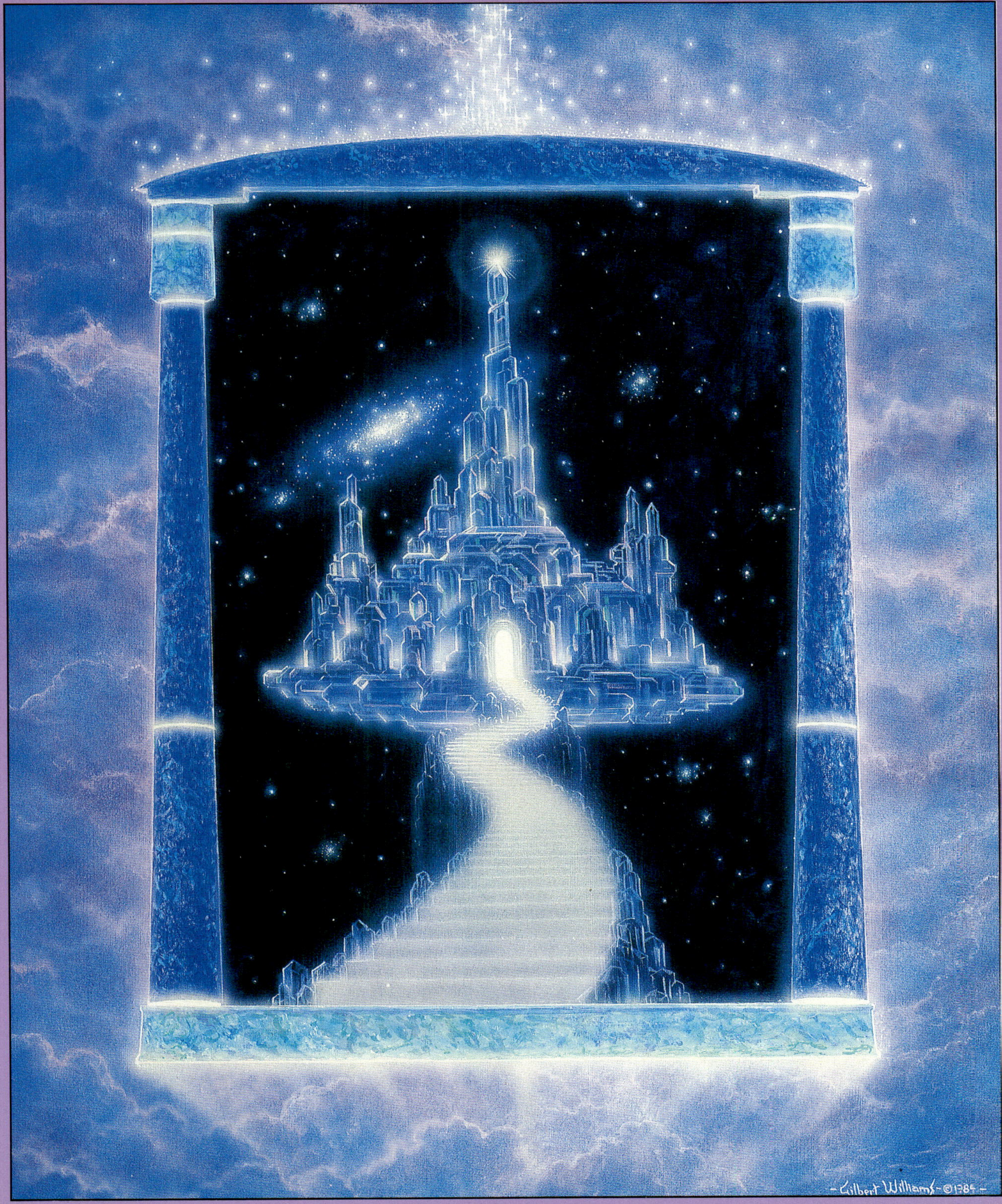
Gilbert Williams

13. DESCENT OF SPRING

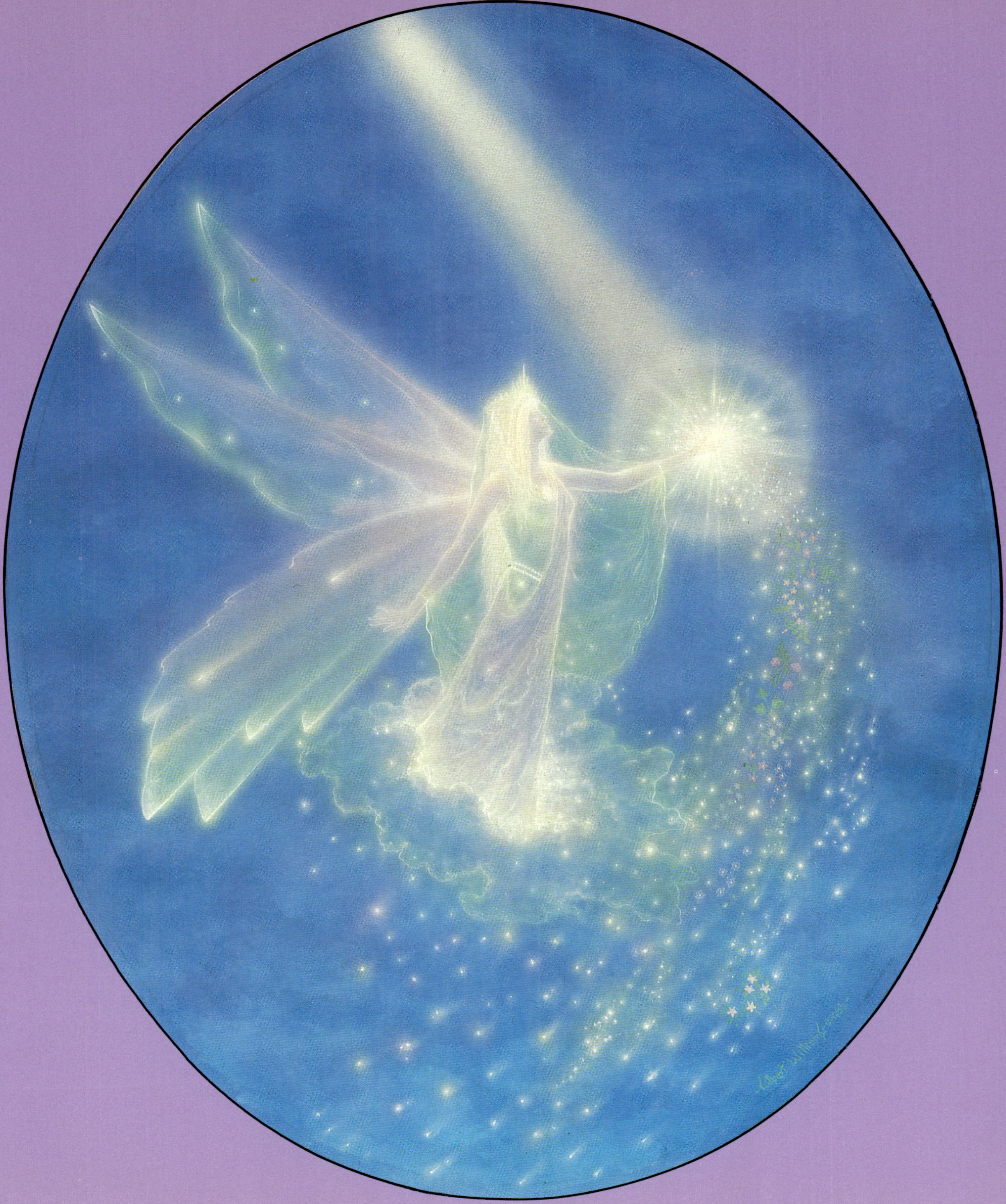

14. ENDLESS JOURNEY

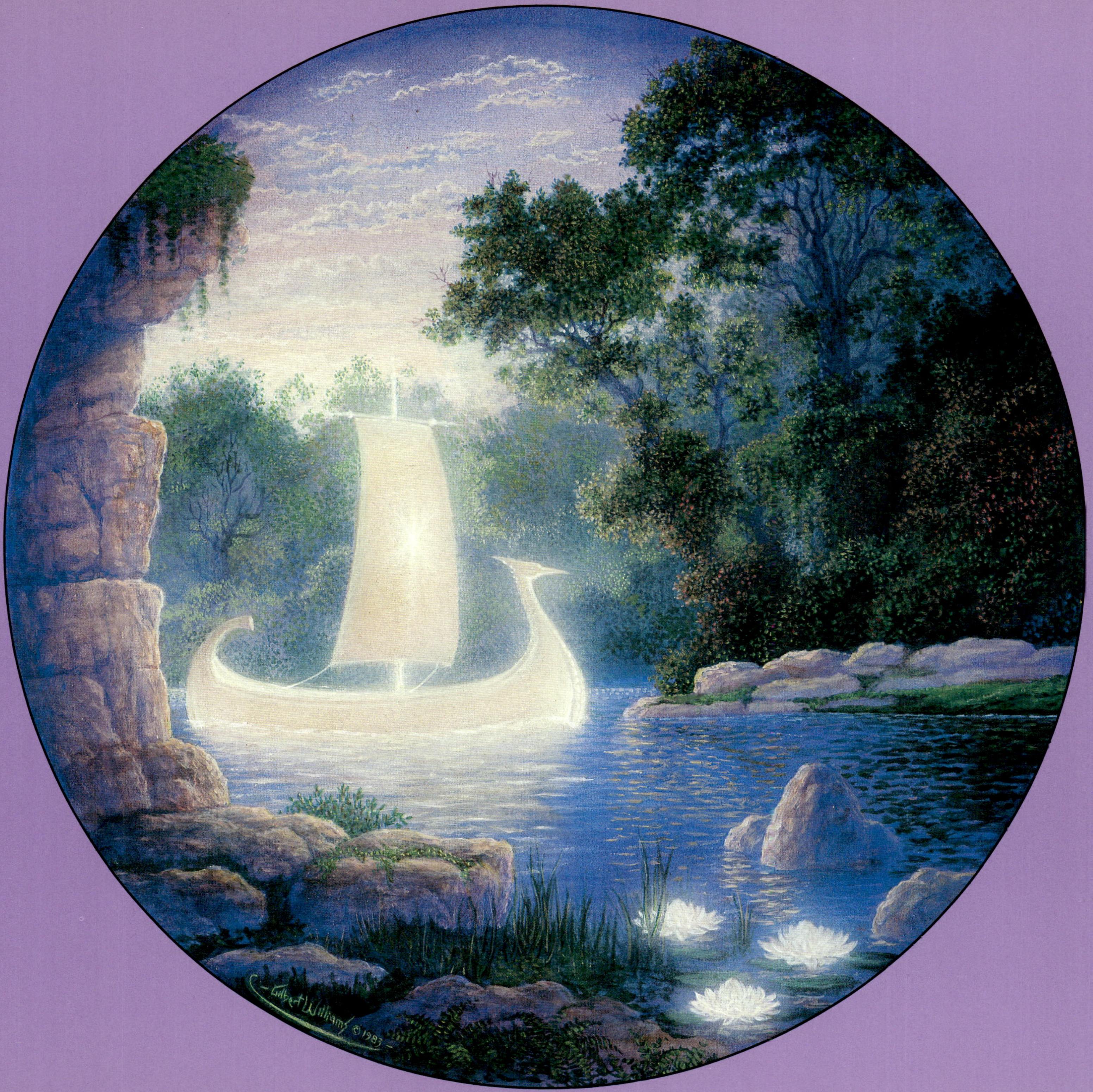
Gilbert Williams ©1983

15. GARDEN OF THE SPHINX

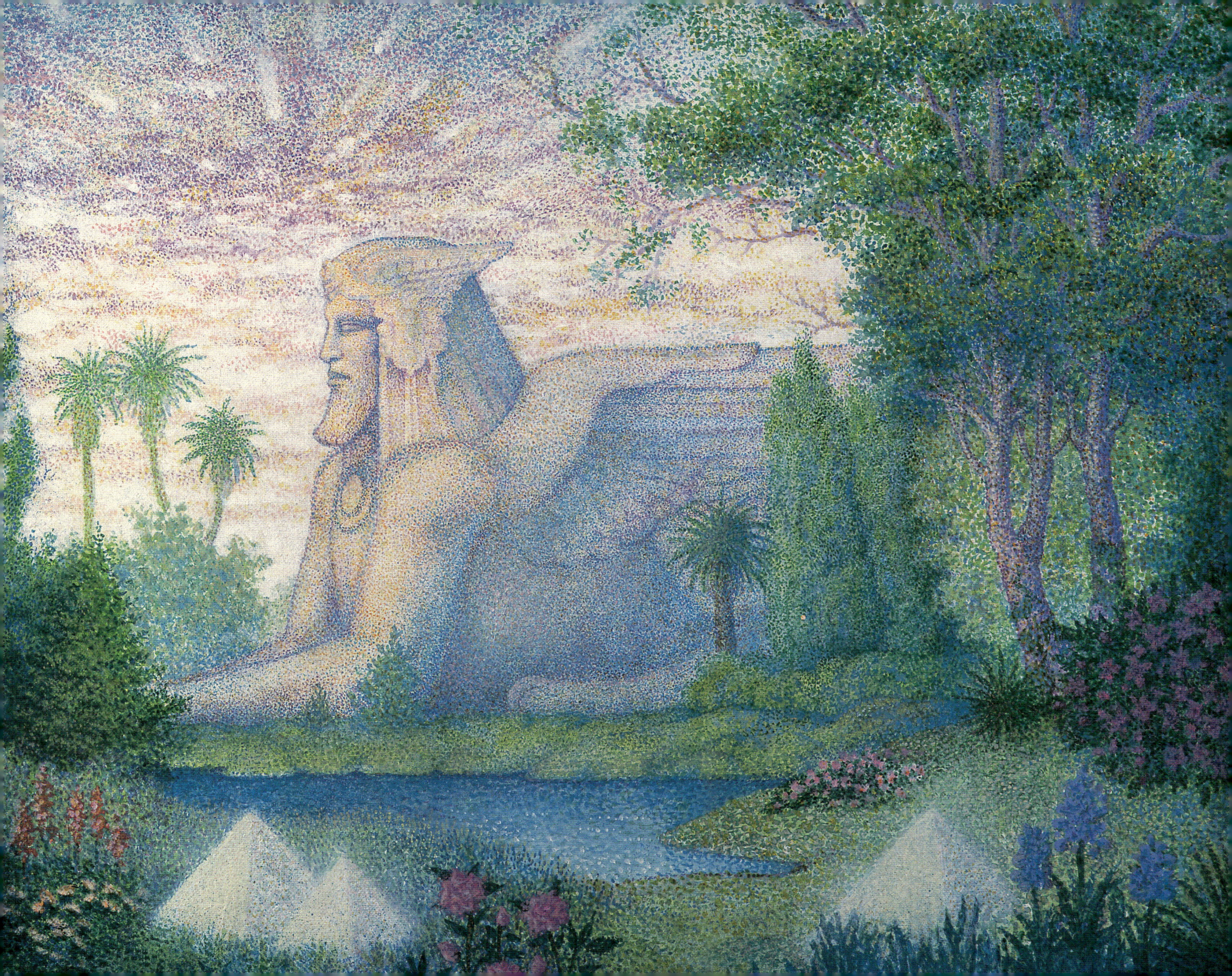

16. GATEWAY

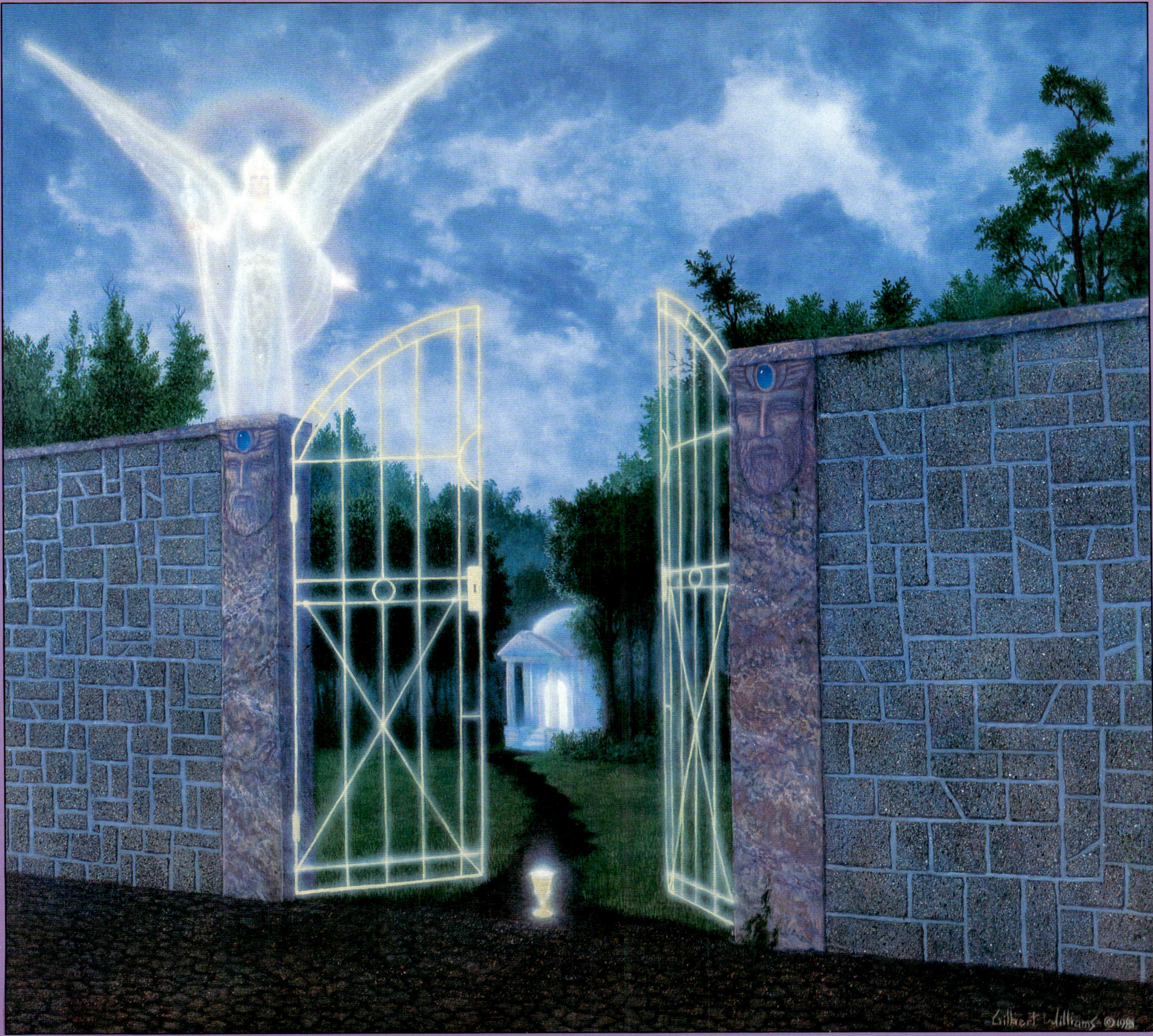
Gilbert Williams

17. GOLDEN TEMPLE

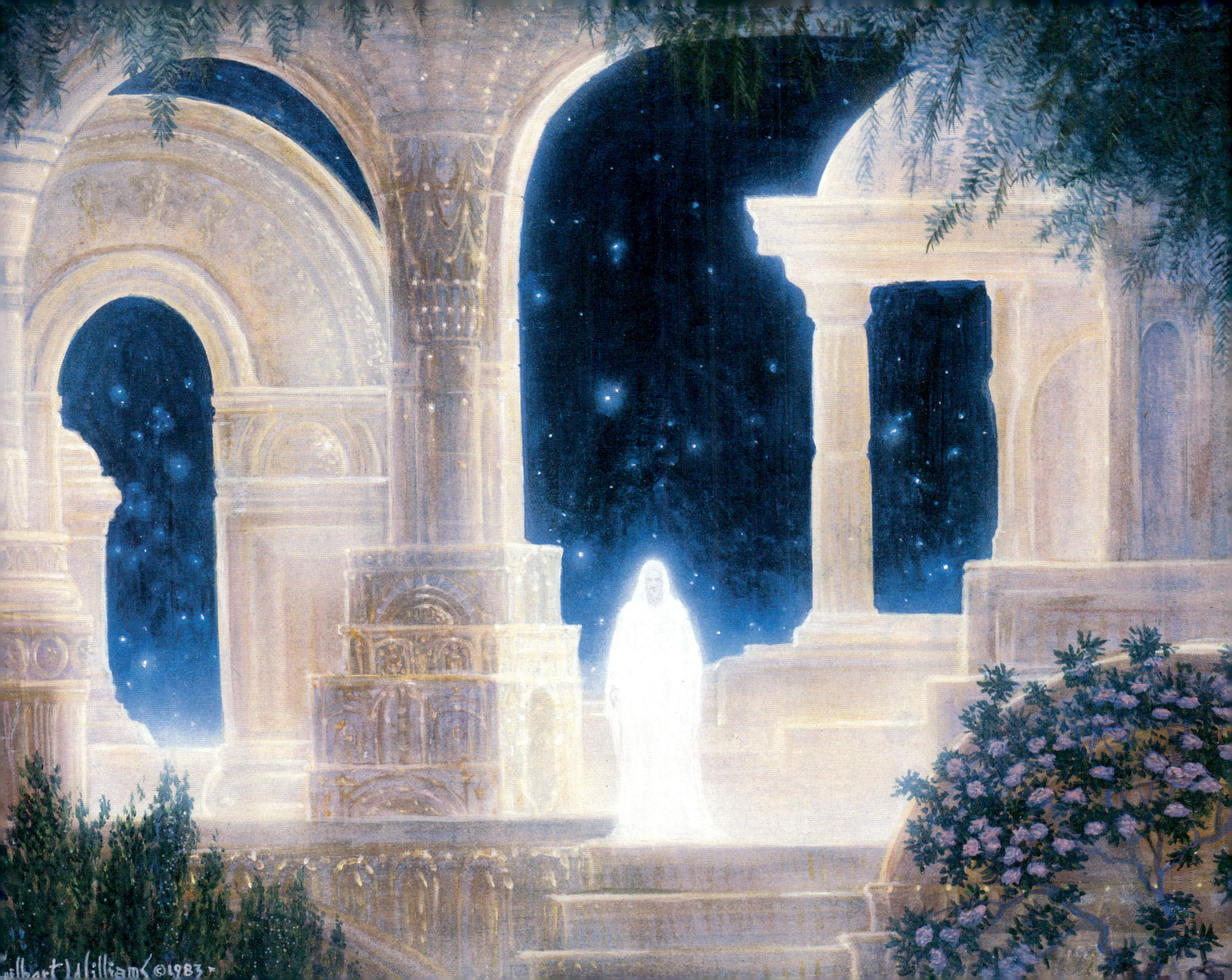
Williams ©1983

18. GUARDIANS OF THE GROVE

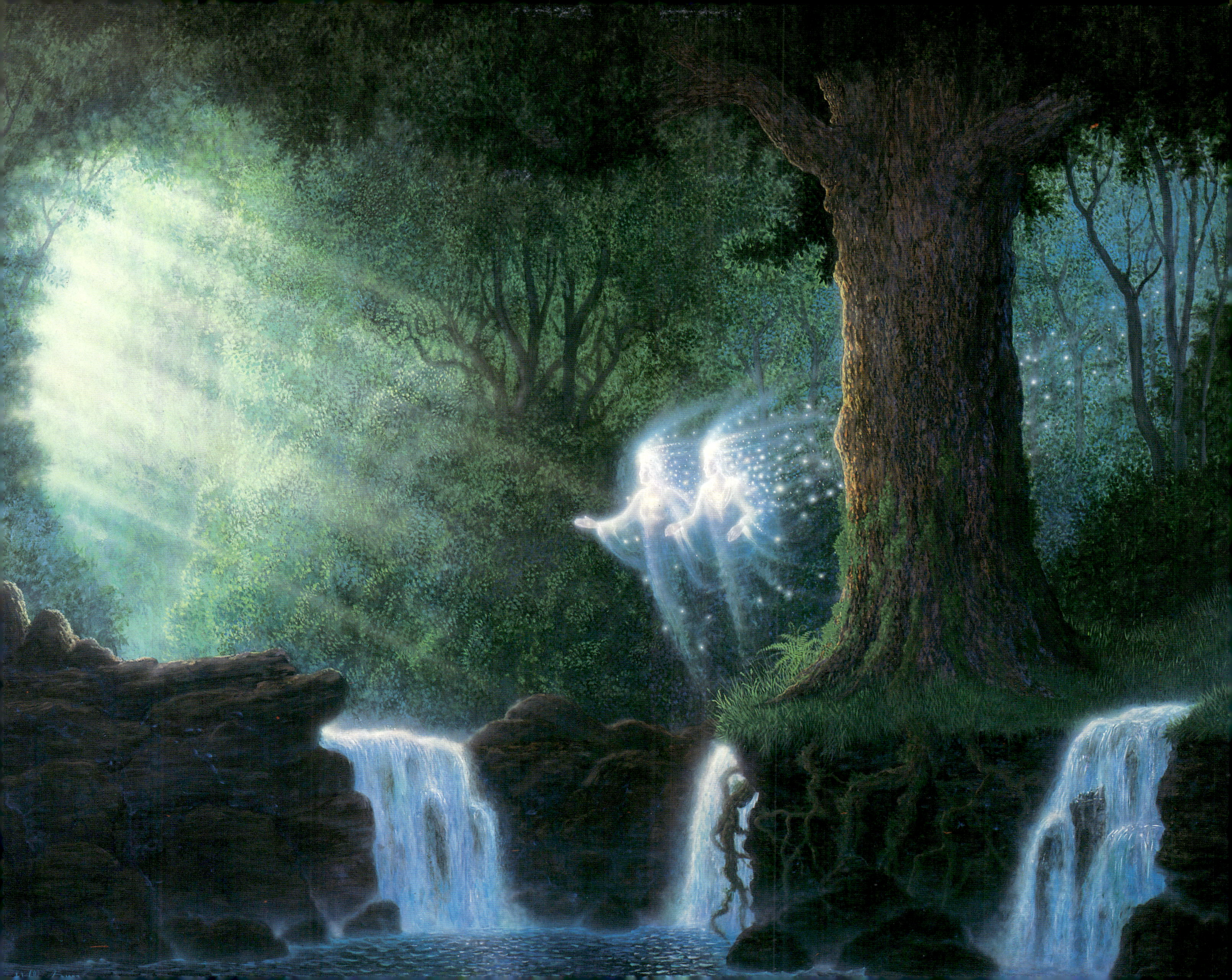

19. INTROSPECTOR

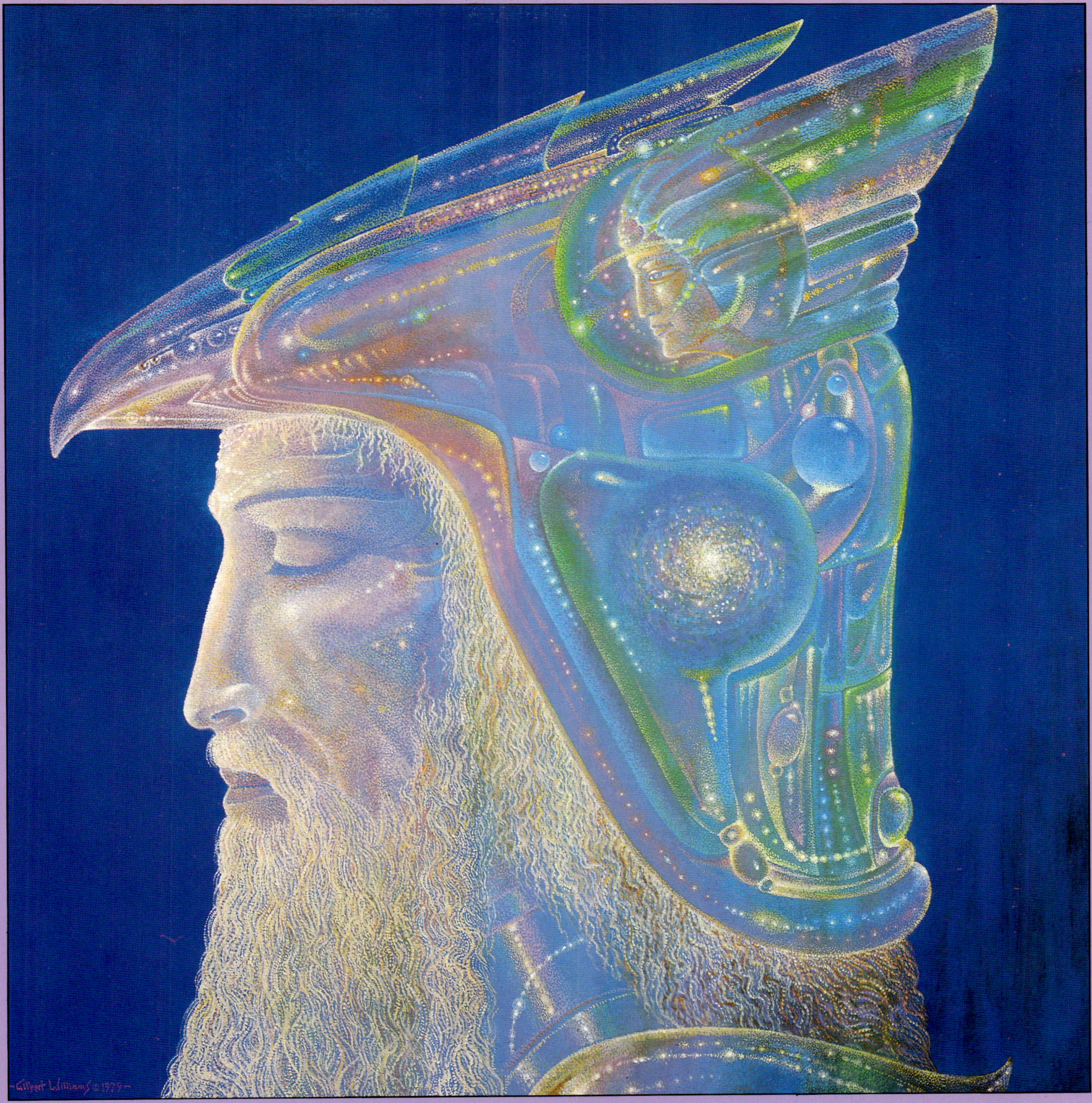
-Gilbert Williams © 1979-

20. ISIS

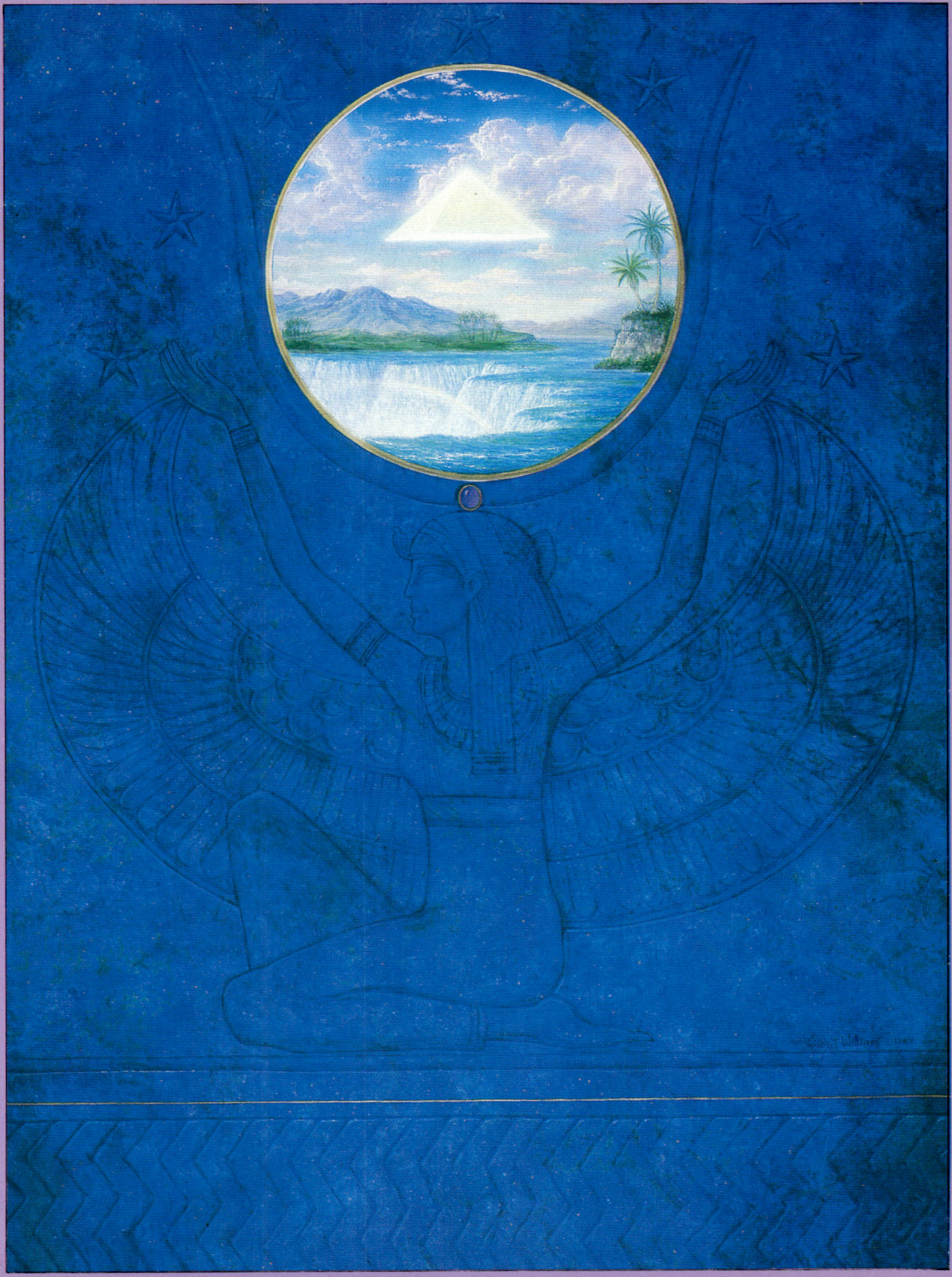

21. LAPIS PYRAMID

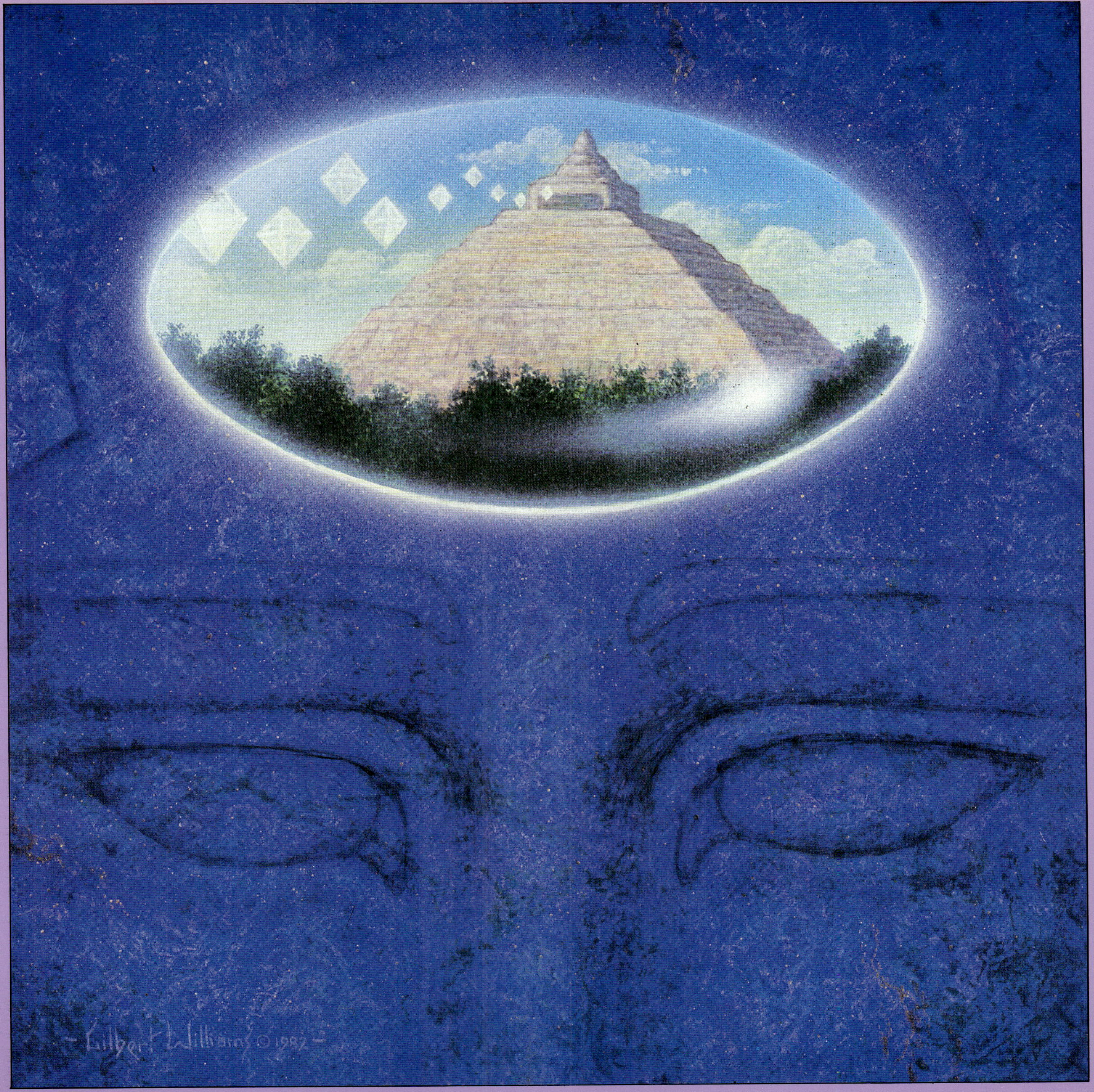
Gilbert Williams © 1982

22. LAZARIS

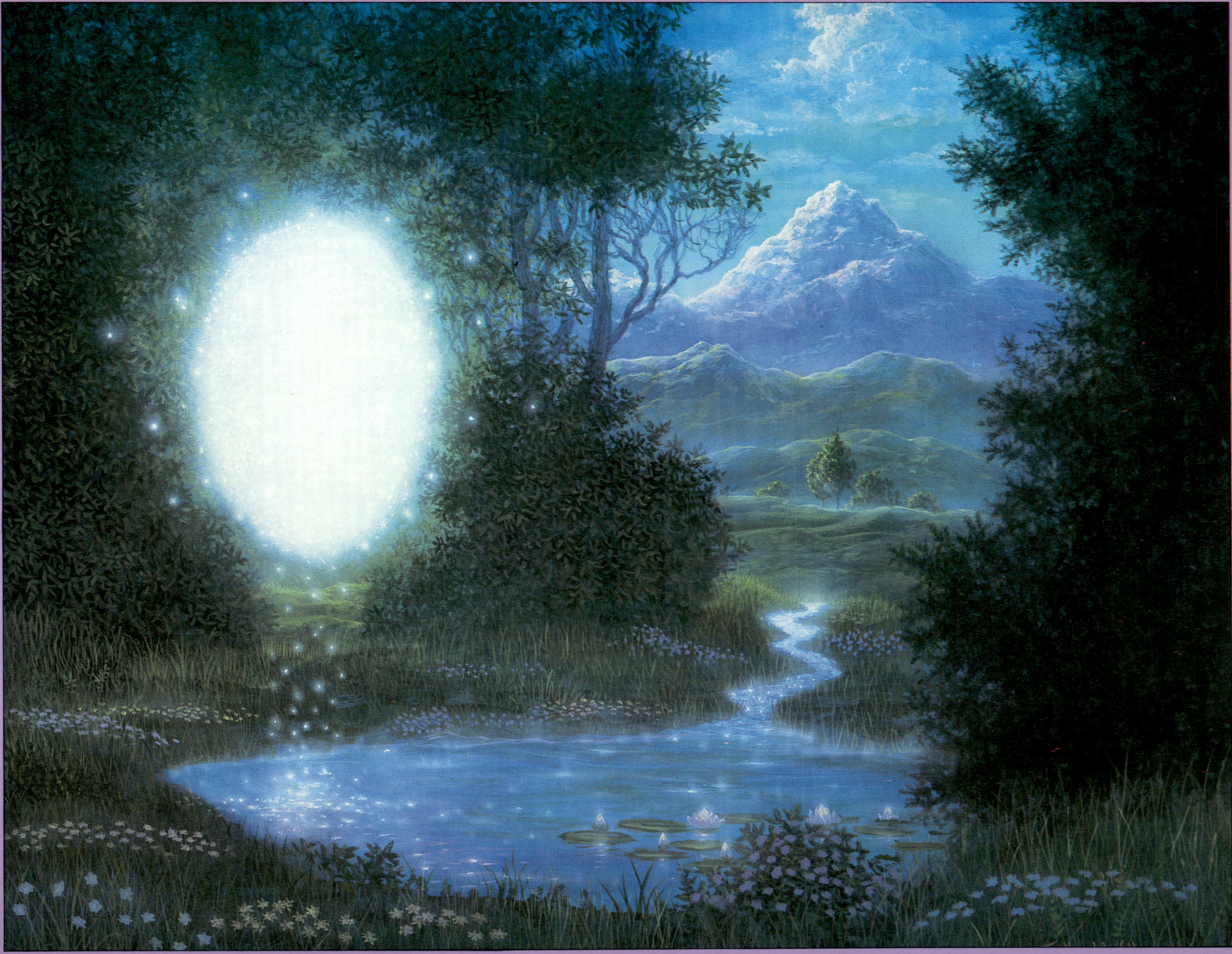

23. MAGICIAN'S GARDEN

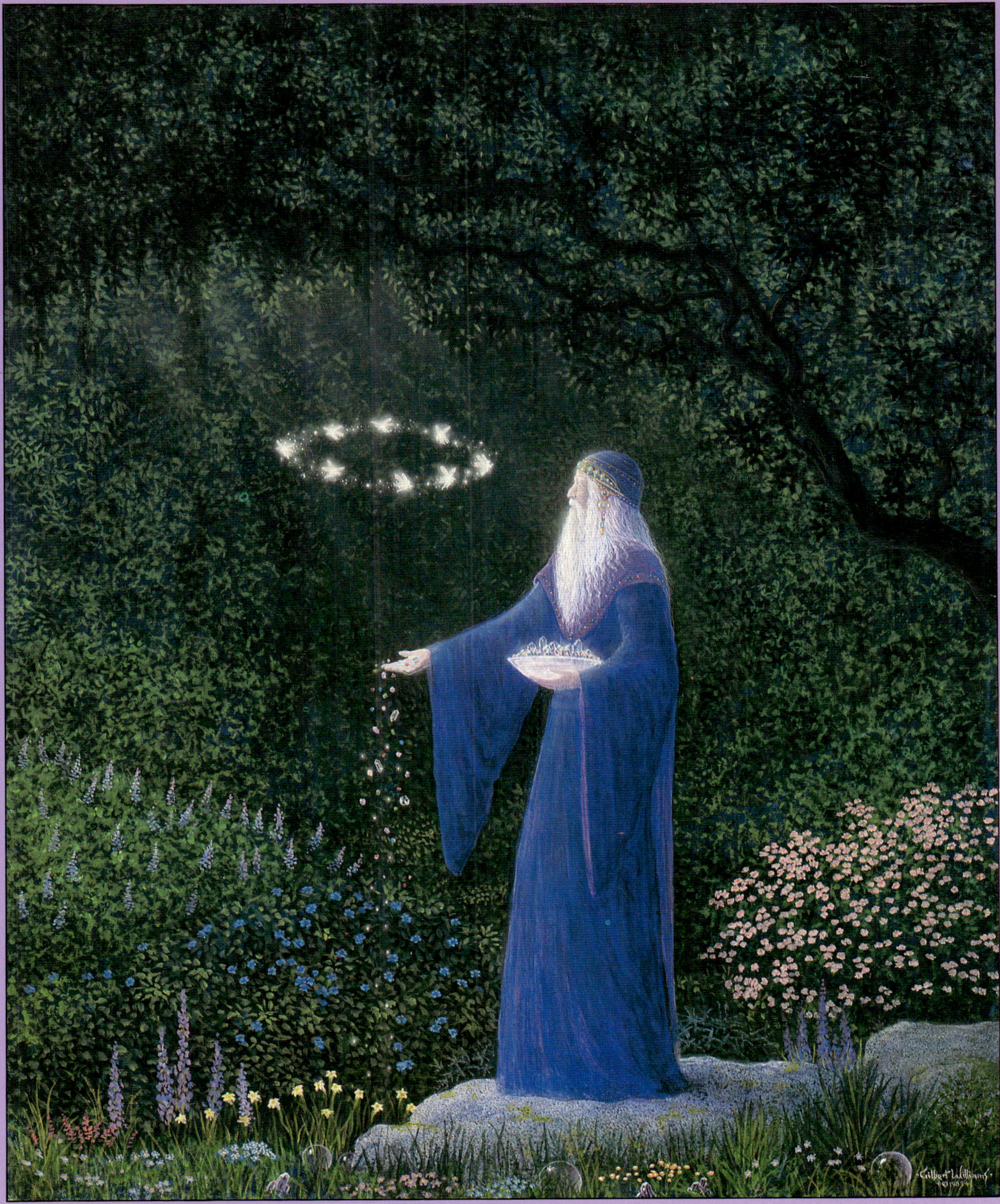
Gilbert Williams
©1983

24. MAGICIAN'S WELL

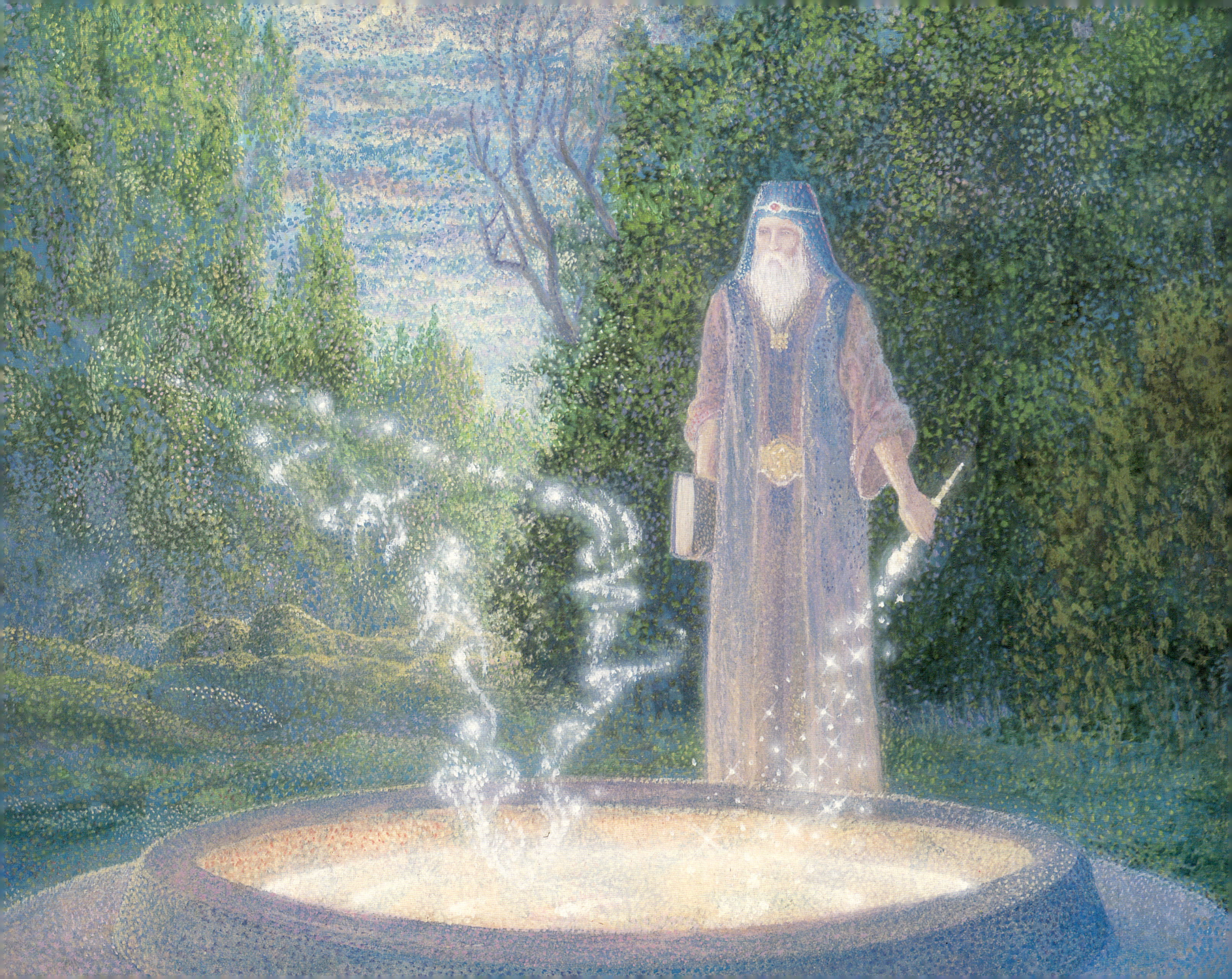

25. MOON DANCERS

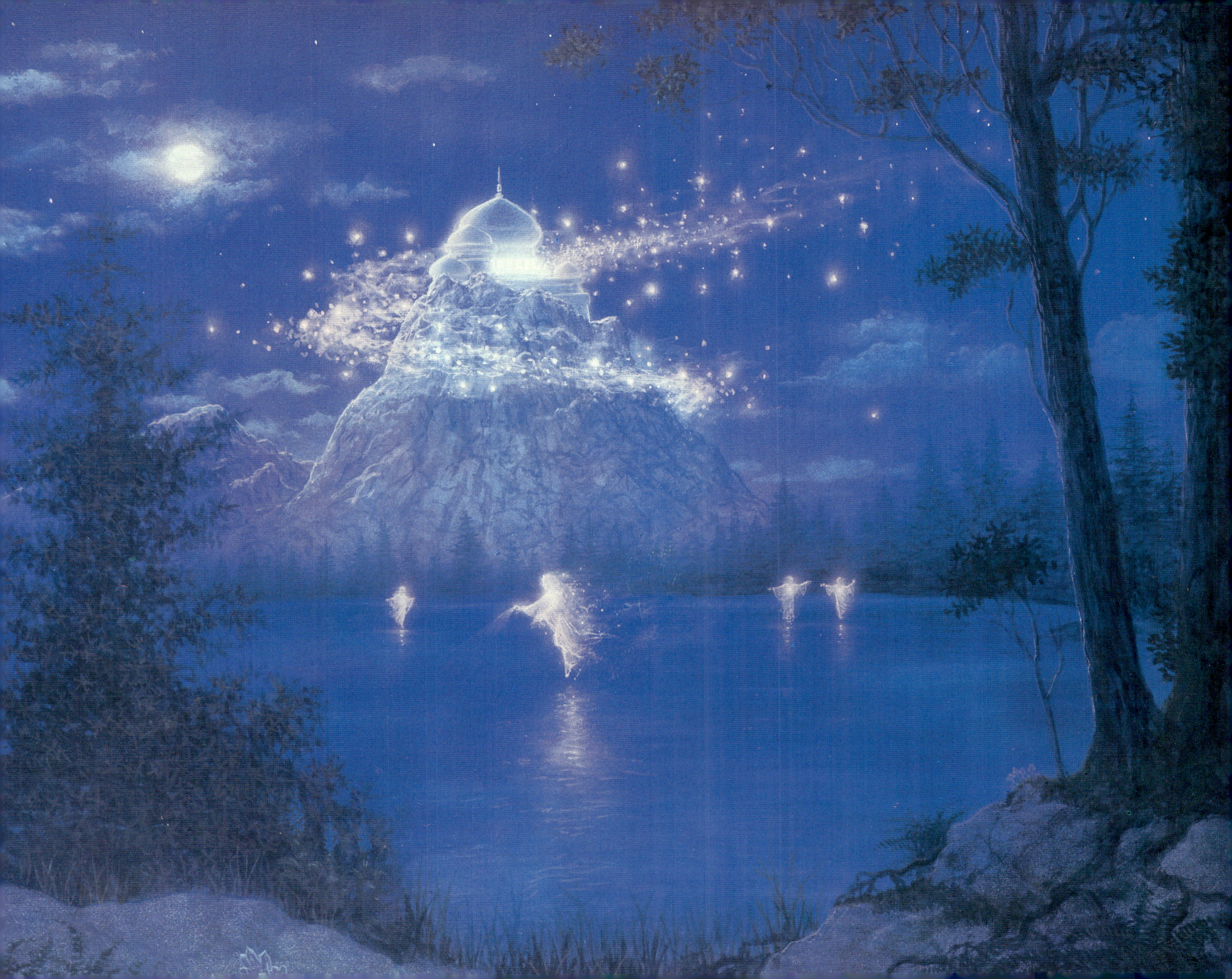

26. MOON TEMPLE

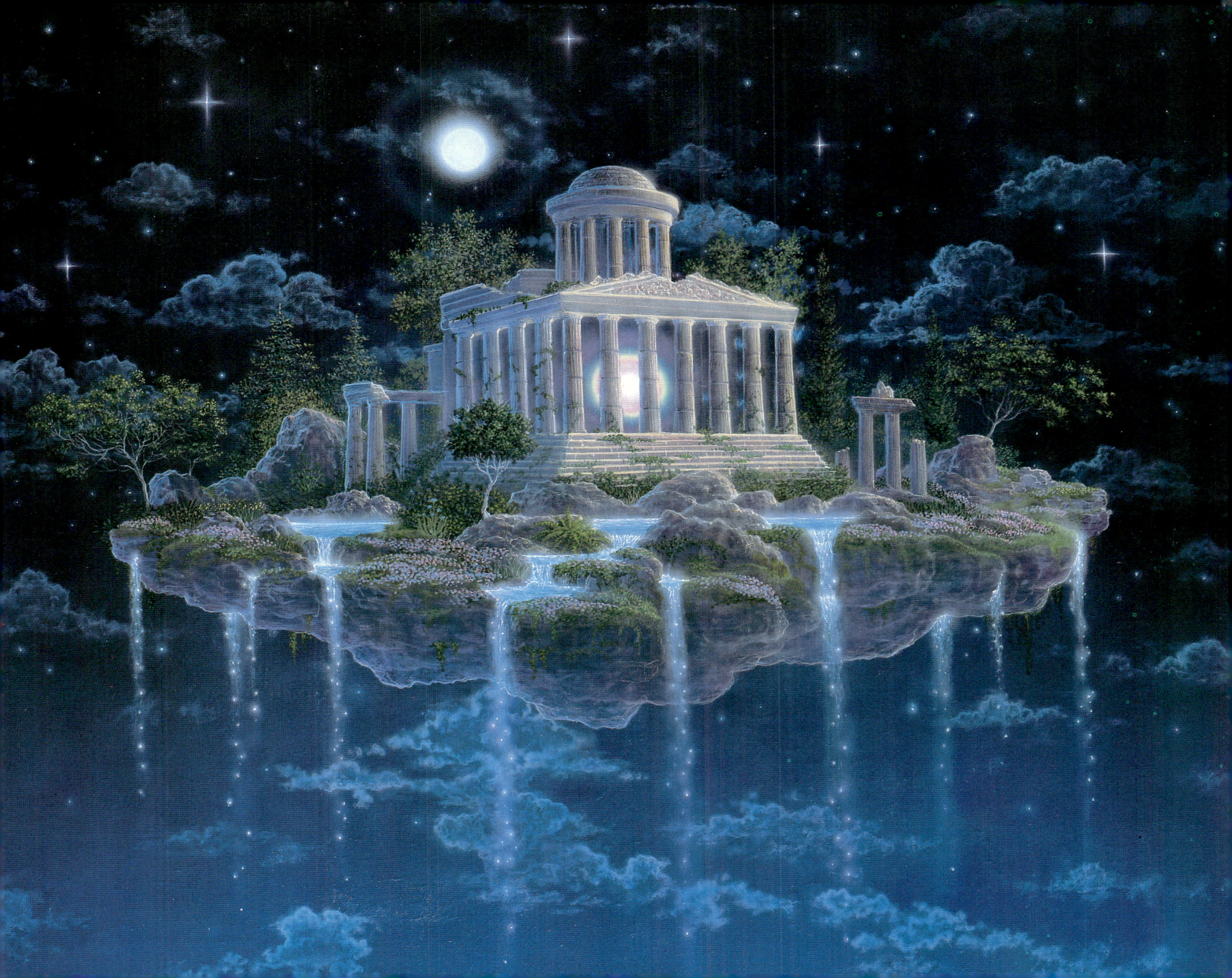

27. MOUNTAIN LIGHTS

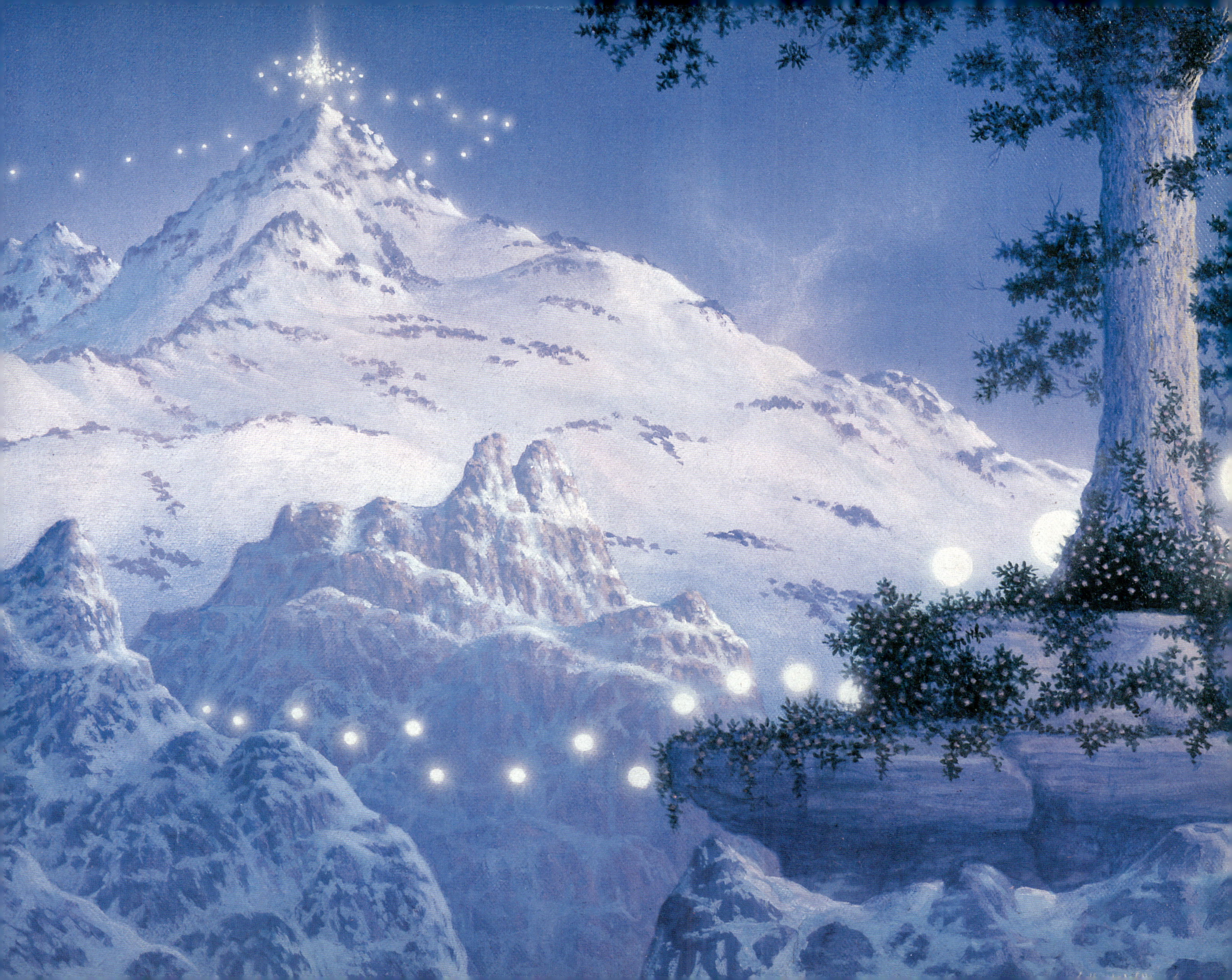

28. ODYSSEY

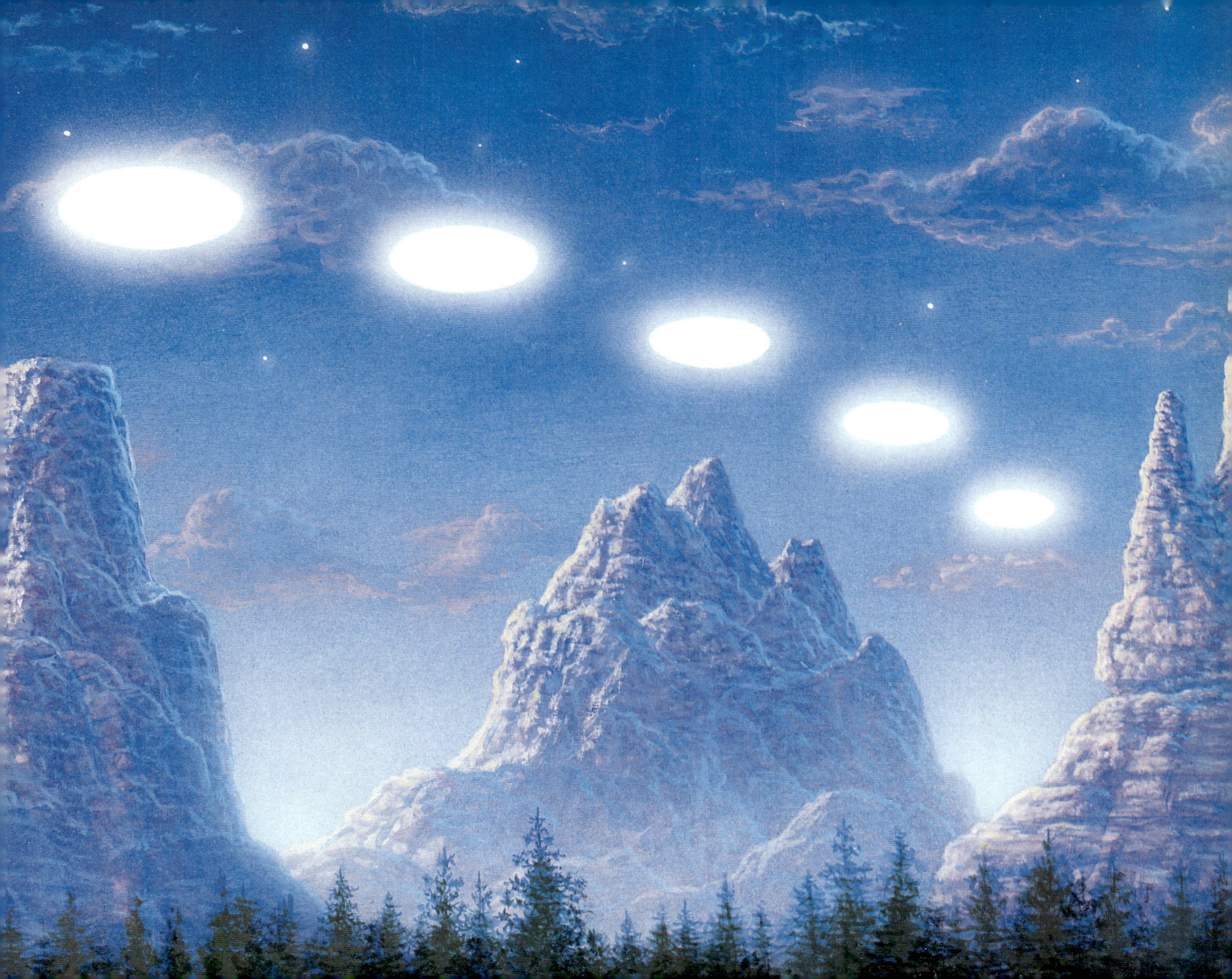

29. OLD MAN

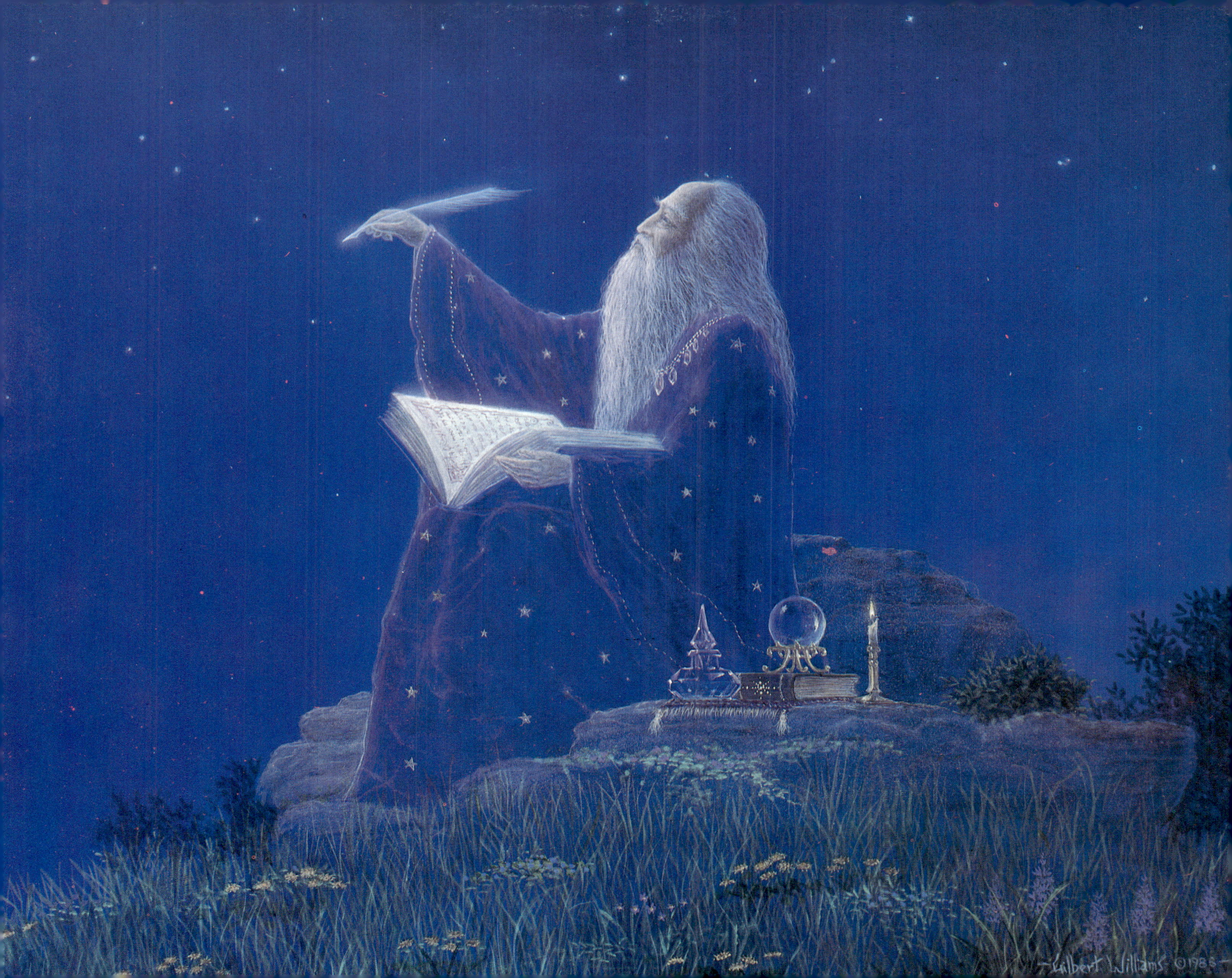
Gilbert Williams

30. PASSAGE

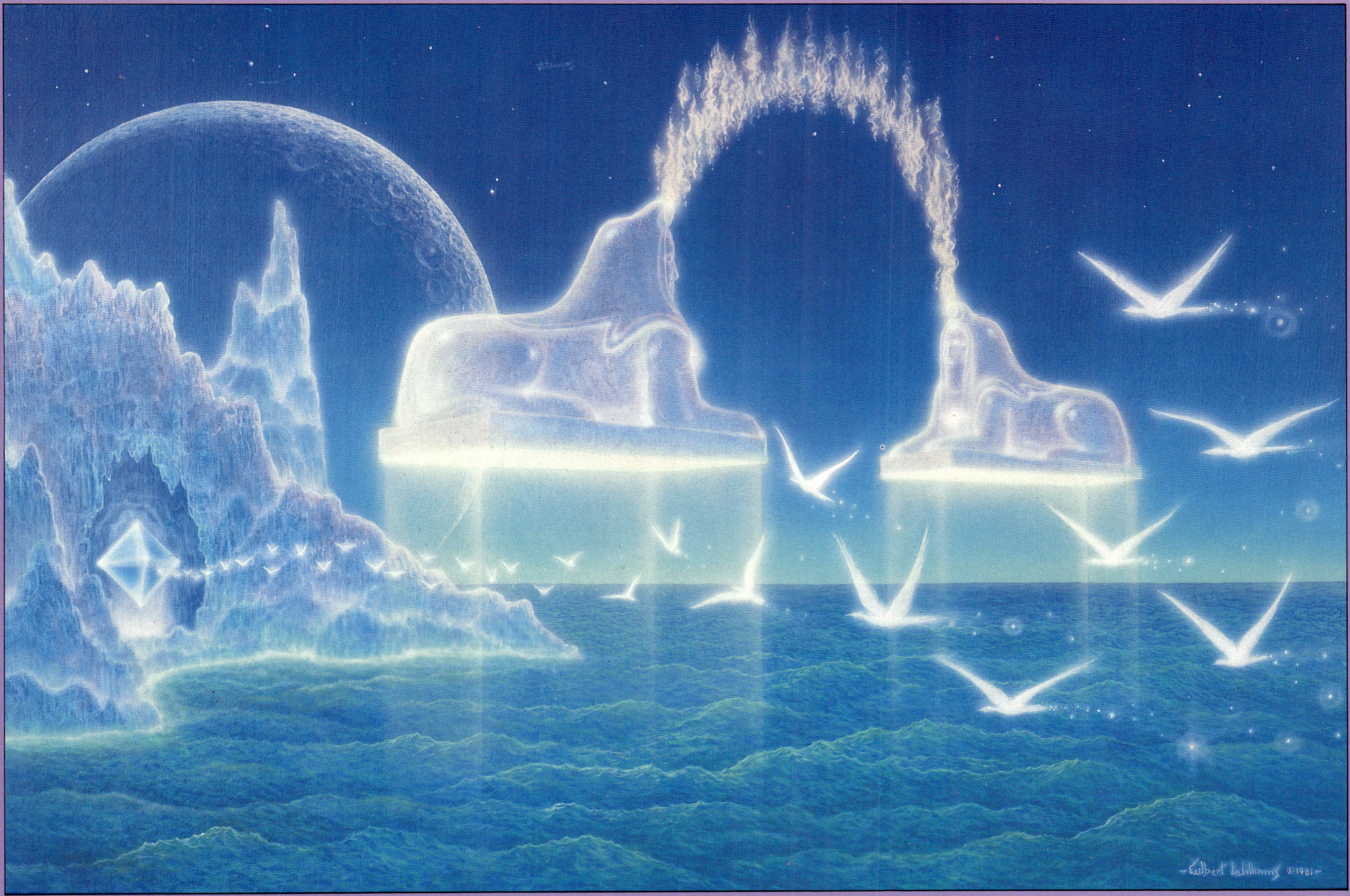
Gilbert Williams ©1981

31. REFLECTIONS

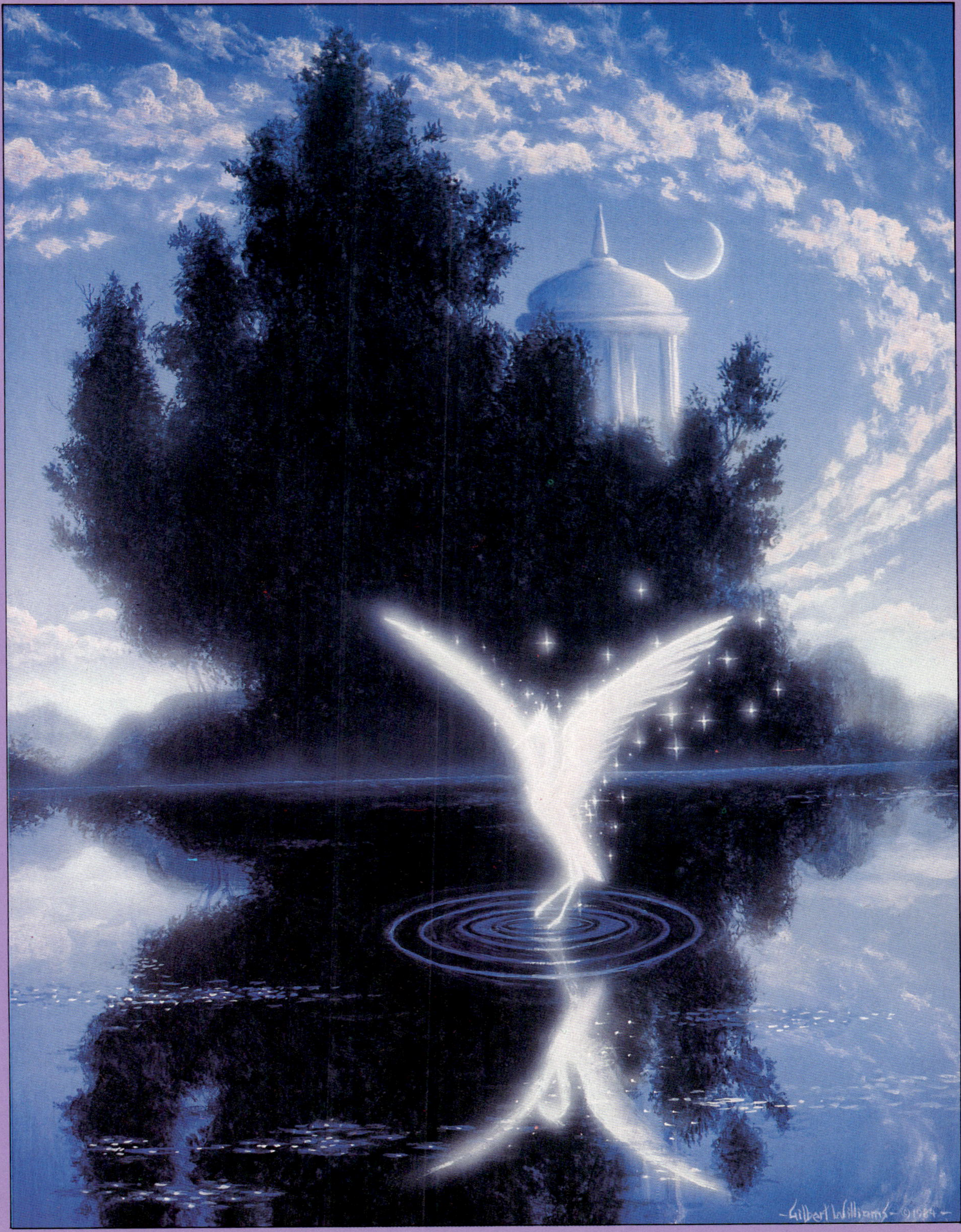
Gilbert Williams ©1984

32. RESURRECTION

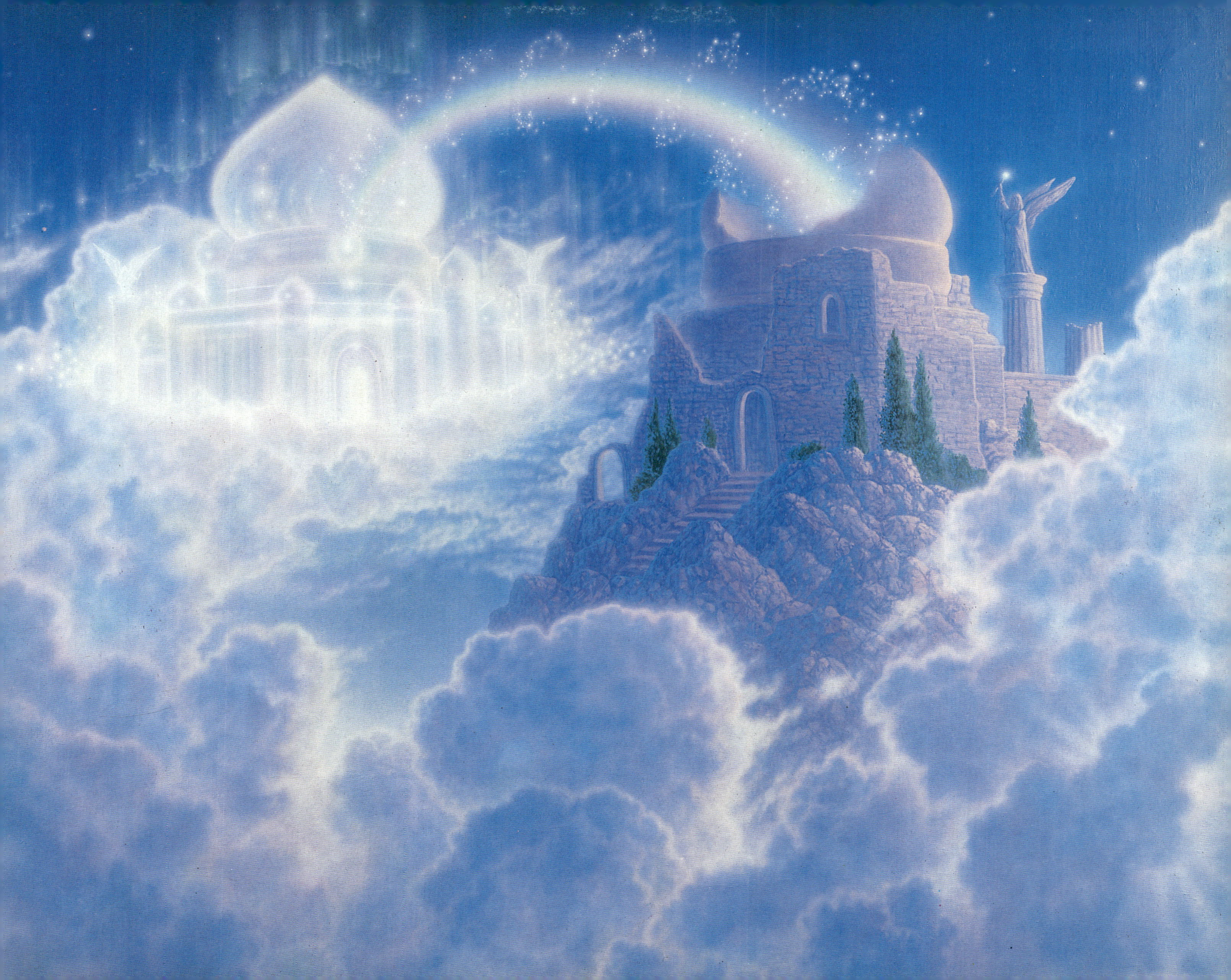

33. SONG OF THE NATURE SPIRITS

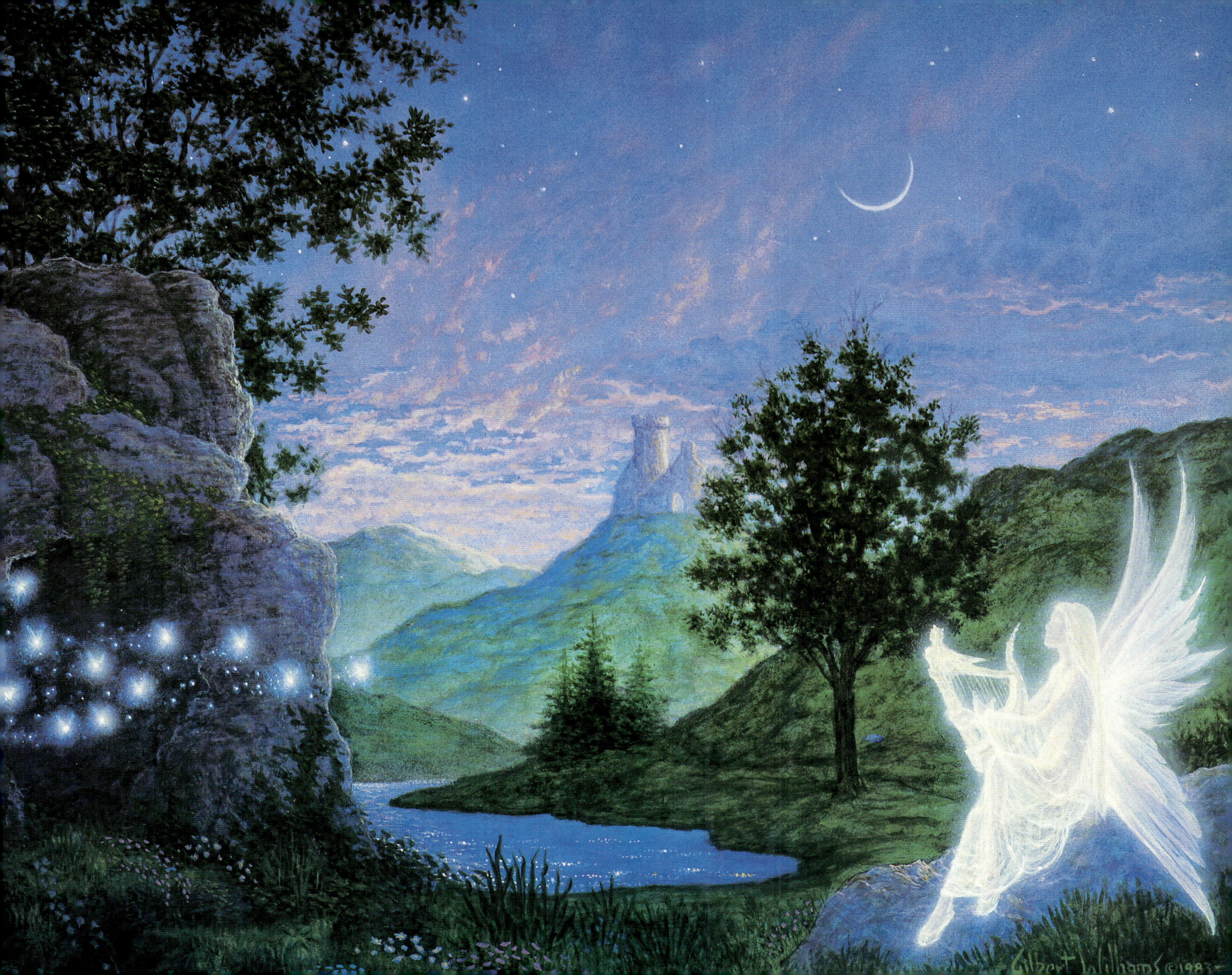

34. SPIRIT OF THE WOOD

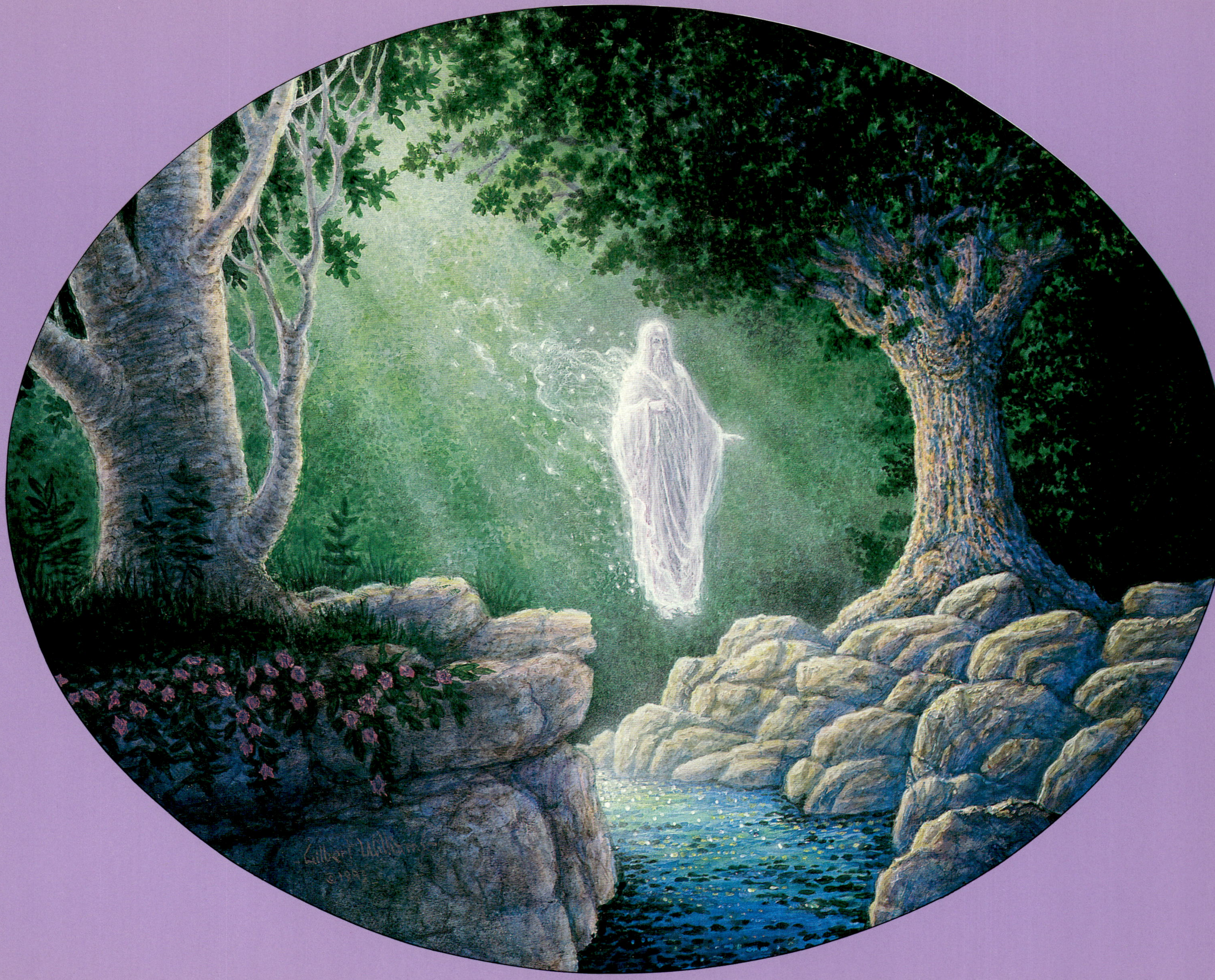

35. SPRING OF WISDOM

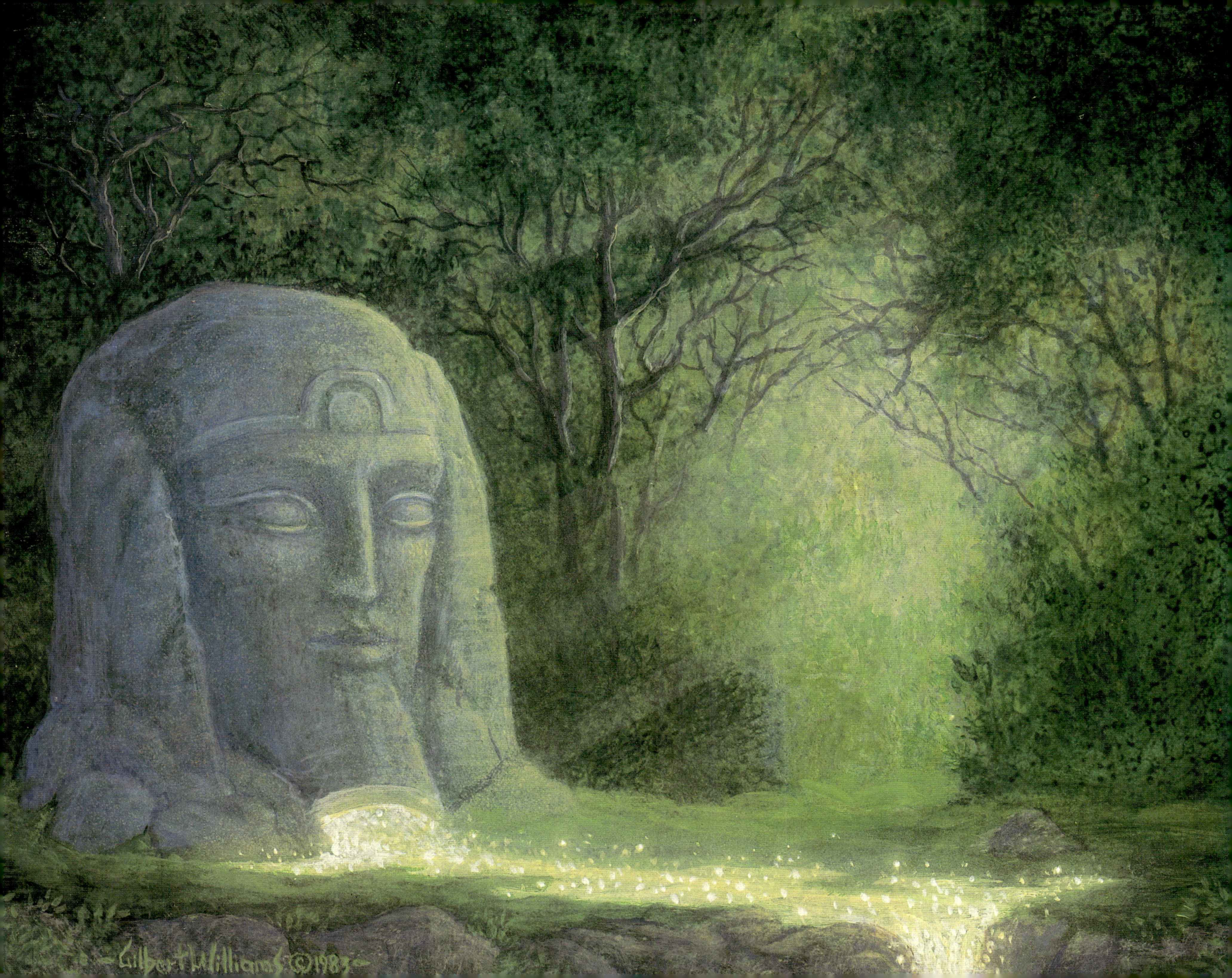
Gilbert Williams ©1983

36. STONE MAN

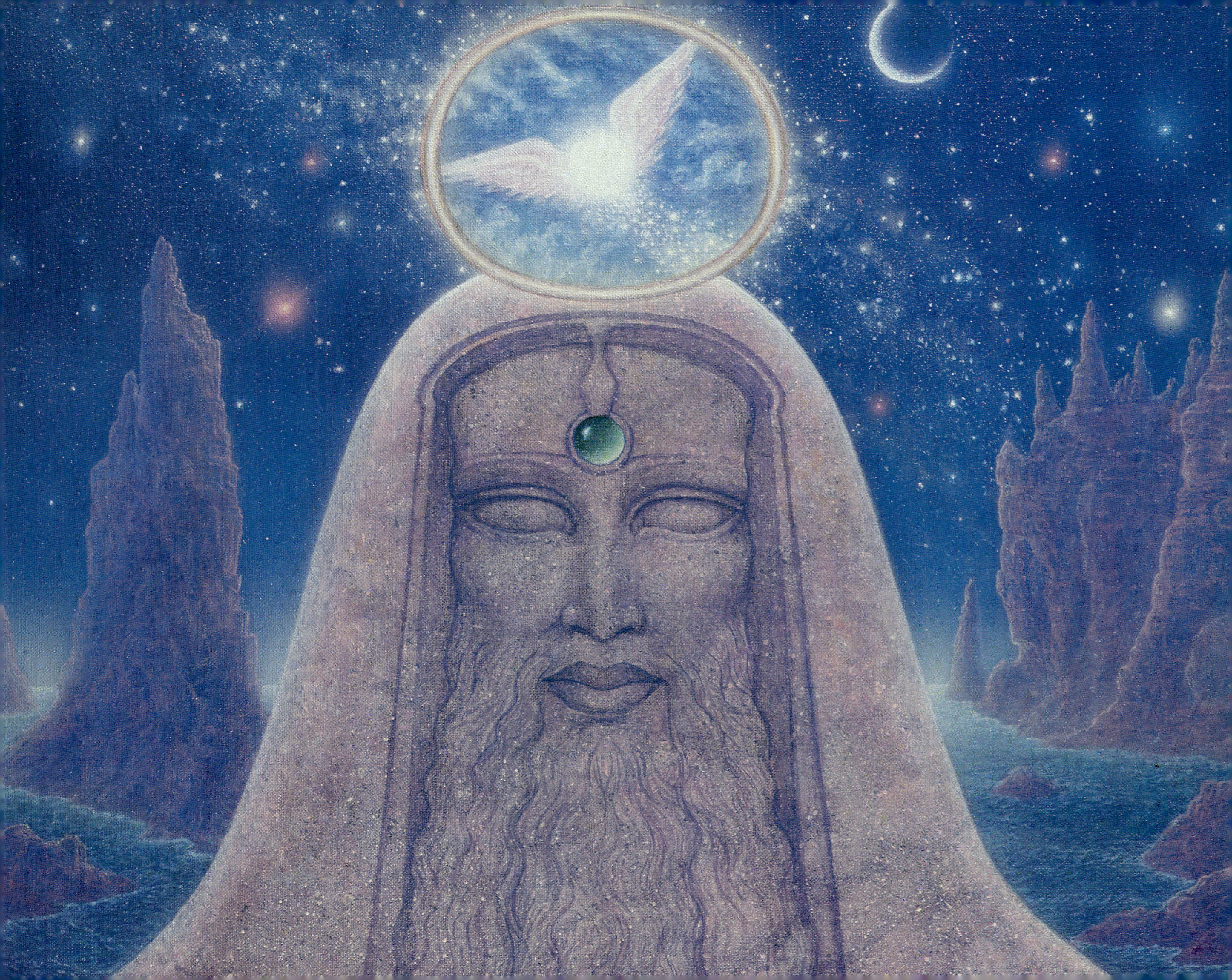

37. SWANS

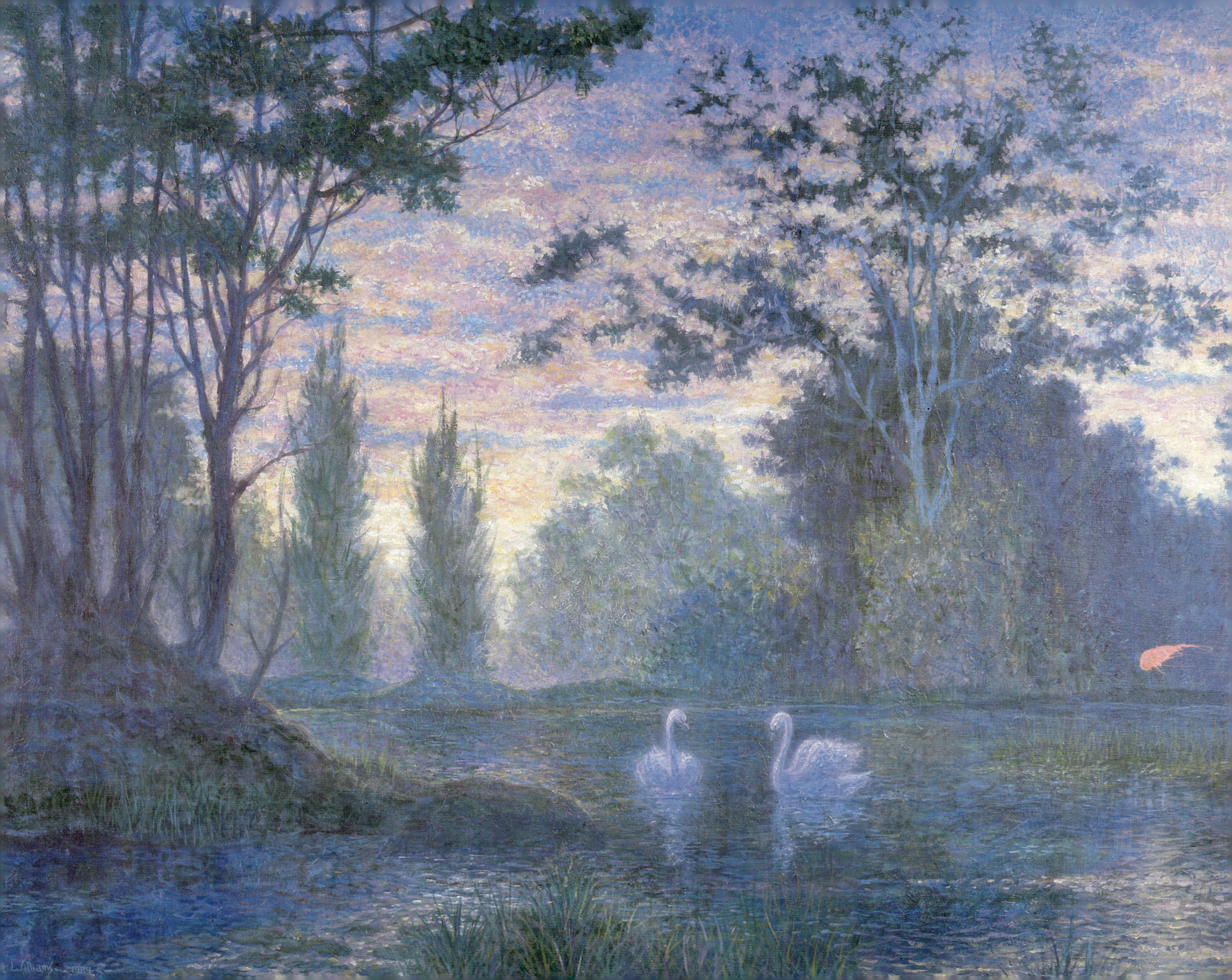

38. TRANSMUTATION

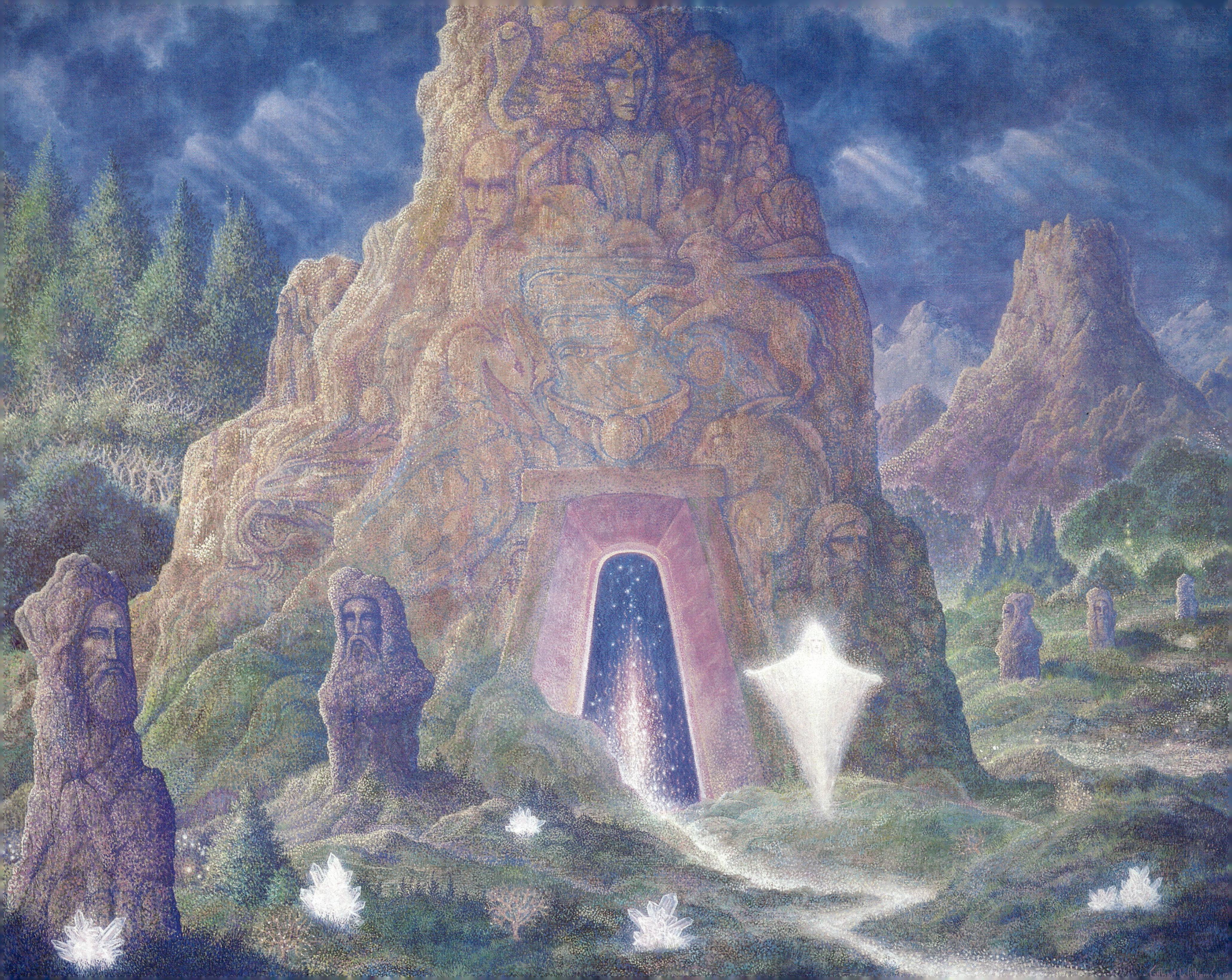

39. WALL OF TEMPLE MYSTERIES

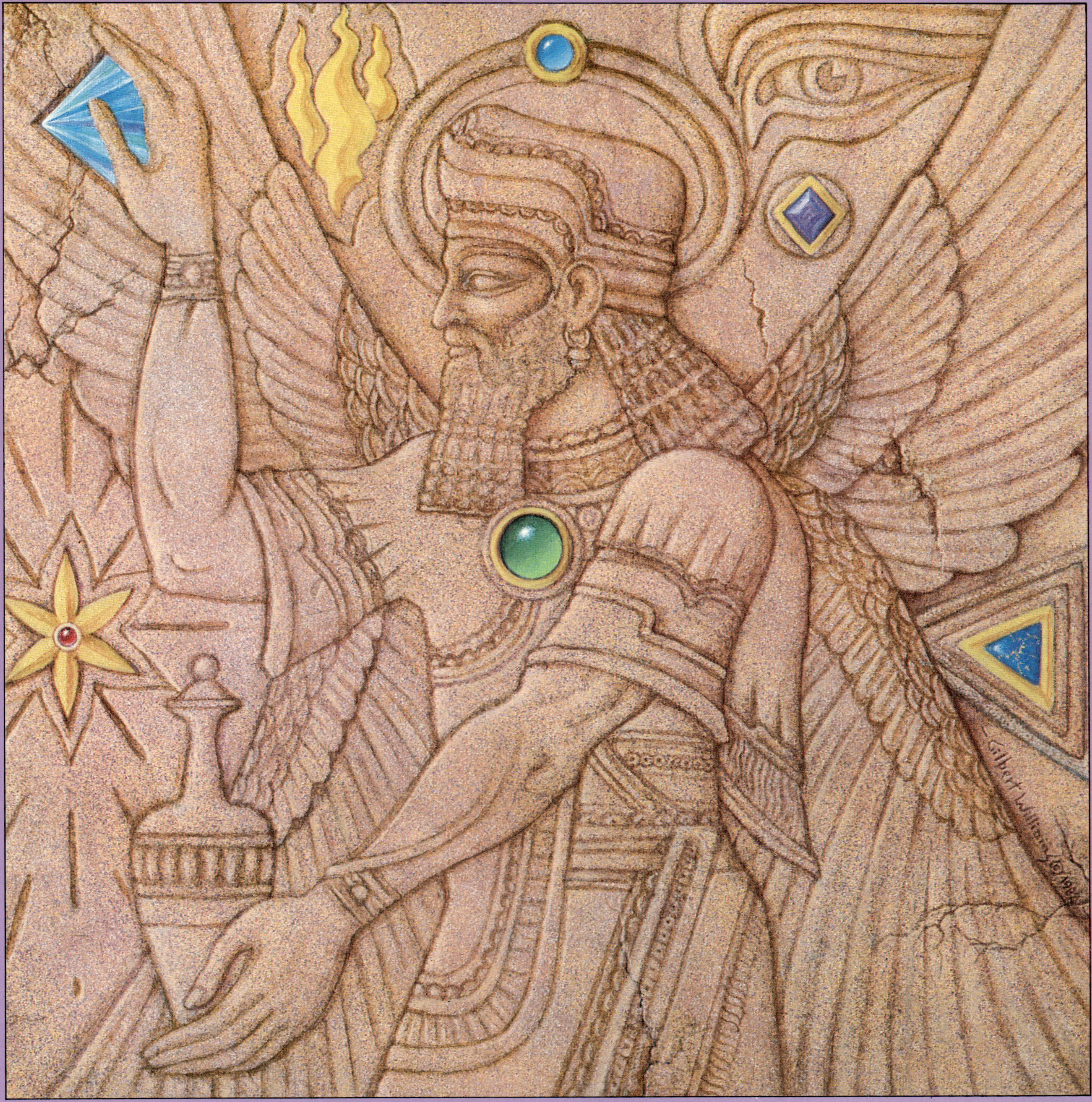
Gilbert Williams

40. WINDOW OF CREATION

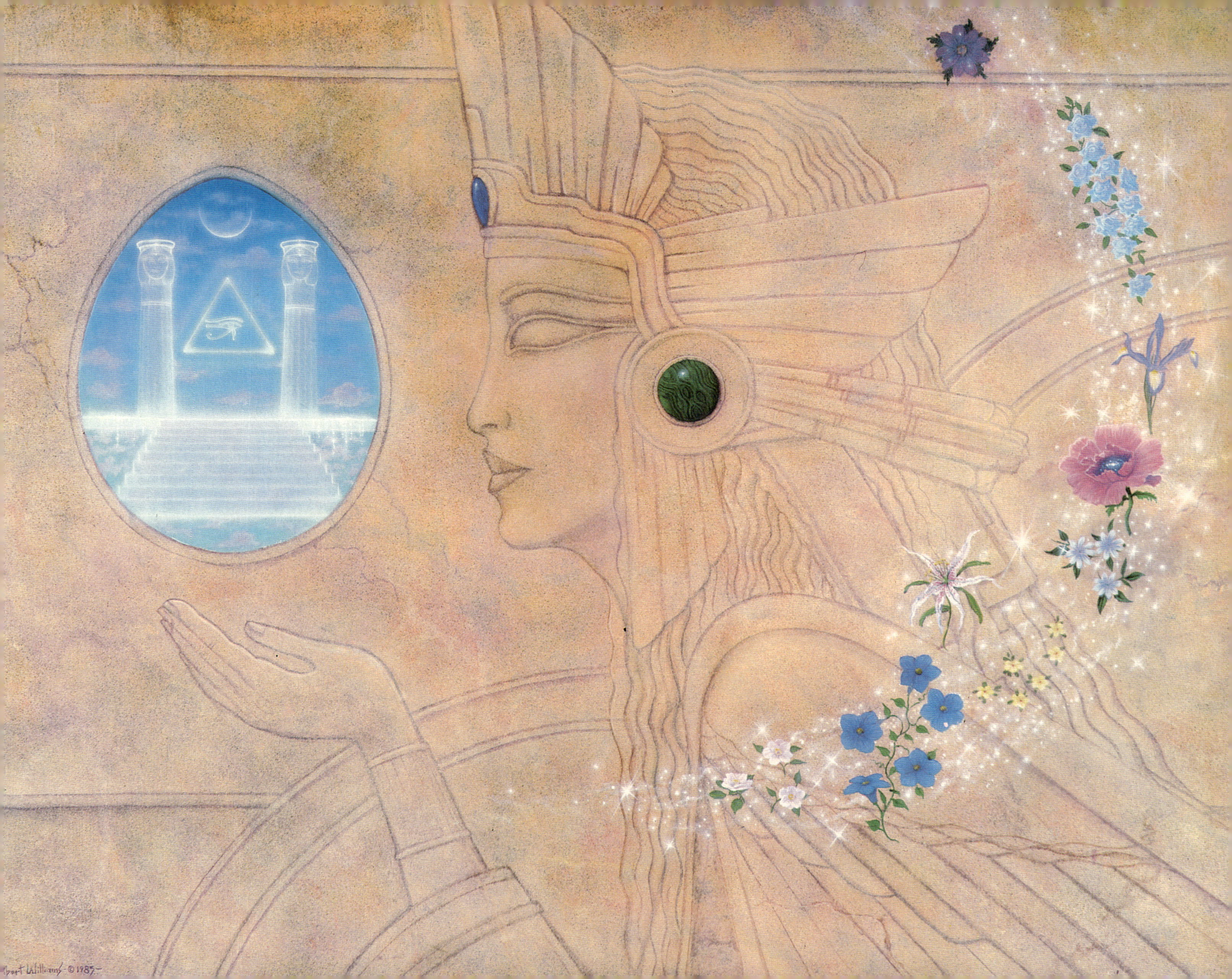
Williams -© 1985-